Richard Harding Davis

The West from a car-window

Richard Harding Davis

The West from a car-window

ISBN/EAN: 9783741113017

Manufactured in Europe, USA, Canada, Australia, Japa

Cover: Foto ©Andreas Hilbeck / pixelio.de

Manufactured and distributed by brebook publishing software (www.brebook.com)

Richard Harding Davis

The West from a car-window

THE WEST
FROM A CAR-WINDOW

BY

RICHARD HARDING DAVIS
AUTHOR OF "VAN BIBBER AND OTHERS" ETC.

ILLUSTRATED

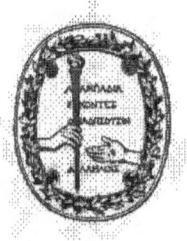

NEW YORK
HARPER & BROTHERS, FRANKLIN SQUARE

Copyright, 1892, by HARPER & BROTHERS.

All rights reserved.

TO
M. K. J.
OF
THE SEVENTH INFANTRY

CONTENTS

	PAGE
FROM SAN ANTONIO TO CORPUS CHRISTI	3
OUR TROOPS ON THE BORDER	27
AT A NEW MINING CAMP	59
A THREE-YEAR-OLD CITY	93
RANCH LIFE IN TEXAS	121
ON AN INDIAN RESERVATION	151
A CIVILIAN AT AN ARMY POST	165
THE HEART OF THE GREAT DIVIDE	215

LIST OF ILLUSTRATIONS

	PAGE
A Bucking Broncho	Frontispiece
Head-piece	3
Rangers in Camp	9
"Remember the Alamo!"	19
Trumpeter Tyler	29
Captain Francis H. Hardie, G Troop, Third United States Cavalry	37
Water	43
The Mexican Guide	49
Third Cavalry Troopers—Searching a Suspected Revolutionist	53
Mining Camp on the Range Above Creede	60
Creede	63
How Land is Claimed for Building—Planks Nailed Together and Resting on Four Stumps	66
The "Holy Moses" Mine	69
Debatable Ground—A Warning to Trespassers	73
A Mining Camp Court-house	75
Shaft of a Mine	79
Valuable Real Estate	83
Upper Creede	87
Oklahoma City on the Day of the Opening	94
Five Days After the Opening	97
Four Weeks After the Opening	101
Captain D. F. Stiles	105
Post-office, April 22, 1889	108

List of Illustrations

	PAGE
Post-office, July 4, 1890	111
Oklahoma City To-day—Main Broadway	115
The Ranch-house on the King Ranch, the Largest Range Owned by One Individual in the United States	123
A Shattered Idol	127
Snapping a Rope on a Horse's Foot	130
Hillingdon Ranch	133
Fixing a Break in the Wire Fence	137
Gathering the Rope	141
Reaction Equals Action	145
Tail-piece	148
The Cheyenne Type	152
Big Bull	155
One of Williamson's Stages	159
The Beef Issue at Anadarko	163
Indian Boy and Pinto Pony	169
A Kiowa Maiden	175
A One-company Post at Oklahoma City	187
The Omnipotent Bugler	191
United States Military Post at San Antonio	195
United States Cavalryman in Full Dress	199
United States Military Post—Infantry Parade	203
Fort Houston, at San Antonio—Officers' Quarters	207
The Barracks, Fort Houston	210
Gateway of the Garden of the Gods, and Pike's Peak	217
Within the Gates, Garden of the Gods	223
Polo Above the Snow-line at Colorado Springs	227
Mount of the Holy Cross	233
Pike's Peak from Colorado Springs	239

I

FROM SAN ANTONIO TO CORPUS CHRISTI

THE WEST FROM A CAR WINDOW
By Richard Harding Davis.

I

FROM SAN ANTONIO TO CORPUS CHRISTI

IT is somewhat disturbing to one who visits the West for the first time with the purpose of writing of it, to read on the back of a railroad map, before he reaches Harrisburg, that Texas "is one hundred thousand square miles larger than all the Eastern and Middle States, including Maryland and Delaware." It gives him a sharp sensation of loneliness, a wish to apologize to some one, and he is moved with a sudden desire to get out at the first station and take the next train back, before his presumption is discovered. He might possibly feel equal to the fact that Texas is "larger than all of the Eastern and Middle States," but this easy addition of one hundred thousand square miles, and the casual throwing in of Maryland and Delaware like potatoes on a basket for good measure, and just as though one or two States more or less did not matter, make him wish he had sensibly confined his observations to that part of the world bounded by Harlem and the Battery.

If I could travel over the West for three years, I might write of it with authority; but when my time is limited to three months, I can only give impressions from a car-window point of view, and cannot dare to draw conclusions. I know that this is an evident and cowardly attempt to "hedge" at the very setting forth. But it is well to understand what is to follow. All that I may hope to do is to tell what impressed an Eastern man in a hurried trip through the Western States. I will try to describe what I saw in such a way that those who read may see as much as I saw with the eyes of one who had lived in the cities of the Eastern States, but the moral they draw must be their own, and can differ from mine as widely as they please.

An Eastern man is apt to cross the continent for the first time with mixed sensations of pride at the size of his country, and shame at his ignorance concerning it. He remembers guiltily how he has told that story of the Englishman who asks the American in London, on hearing he is from New York, if he knows his brother in Omaha, Nebraska. And as the Eastern man finds from the map of his own country that the letters of introduction he has accepted from intelligent friends are addressed to places one and two thousand miles apart, he determines to drop that story about the Englishman, and tell it hereafter at the expense of himself and others nearer home.

His first practical surprise perhaps will be when he discovers the speed and ease with which numerous States are passing under him, and that smooth road-beds and parlor-cars remain with him to the very borders of the West. The change of time will trouble him at first, until he gets nearer to Mexico, when he will have his choice of three separate standards, at which point he will cease winding his watch altogether, and devote his "twenty minutes for refreshments" to watching the conductor. But this minor and merely nominal change will not distress him half so seriously as will the sudden and actual disarrangement of his dinner hour from seven at night to two in the afternoon, though even this will become possible after he finds people in south-western Texas eating duck for breakfast.

He will take his first lesson in the politics of Texas and of the rest of the West when he first offers a ten-dollar bill for a dollar's worth of something, and is given nine large round silver dollars in change. When he has twenty or more of these on his person, and finds that his protests are met with polite surprise, he understands that silver is a large and vital issue, and that the West is ready to suffer its minor disadvantages for the possible good to come.

He will get his first wrong impression of the West through reading the head-lines of some of the papers, and from the class of books offered for sale on the cars and in the hotels and book-stores from St. Louis to Corpus Christi. These head-lines shock even a hardened newspaper man. But they do not represent the feeling of their readers, and in that they give a wrong and unfortunate impression to the visiting stranger. They told while I was in St. Louis of a sleighing party of twenty, of whom nine were instantly killed by a locomotive, and told it as flippantly as though it were a picnic; but the accident itself was the one and serious comment of the day, and the horror of it seemed to have reached every class of citizen.

It is rather more difficult to explain away the books. They are too obvious and too much in evidence to be accidental. To judge from them, one would imagine that Boccaccio, Rabelais, Zola, and such things as *Velvet Vice* and *Old Sleuth*, are all that is known to the South-west of literature. It may be that the booksellers only keep them for their own perusal, but they might have something better for their customers.

The ideas which the stay-at-home Eastern man obtains of the extreme borderland of Texas are gathered from various sources, principally from those who, as will all travellers, make as much of what they have seen as is possible, this much being generally to show the differences which exist between the places they have visited and their own home. Of the similarities they say nothing. Or he has read of the bandits and outlaws of the Garza revolution, and he has seen the Wild West show of the Hon. William F. Cody. The latter, no doubt, surprised and delighted him very much. A mild West show, which would be equally accurate, would surprise him even more; at least, if it was organized in the wildest part of Texas between San Antonio and Corpus Christi.

When he leaves this first city and touches at the border of Mexico, at Laredo, and starts forth again across the prairie of cactus and chaparral towards "Corpus," he feels assured that at last he is done with parlor-cars and civilization; that he is about to see the picturesque and lawless side of the Texan existence, and that he has taken his life in his hands. He will be the more readily convinced of this when the young man with the broad shoulders and sun-browned face and wide sombrero in the seat in front raises the car-window, and begins to shoot splinters out of the passing telegraph poles with the melancholy and listless air of one who is performing a casual divertisement. But he will be better informed when the Chicago drummer has risen hurriedly, with a pale face, and has reported what is going on to the conductor, and he hears that dignitary say, complacently: "Sho! that's only 'Will' Scheeley practisin'! He's a dep'ty sheriff."

From San Antonio to Corpus Christi

He will learn in time that the only men on the borders of Texas who are allowed to wear revolvers are sheriffs, State agents in charge of prisoners, and the Texas Rangers, and that whenever he sees a man so armed he may as surely assume that he is one of these as he may know that in New York men in gray uniforms, with leather bags over their shoulders, are letter-carriers. The revolver is the Texan officer's badge of office; it corresponds to the New York policeman's shield; and he toys with it just as the Broadway policeman juggles his club. It is quite as harmless as a toy, and almost as terrible as a weapon.

This will grieve the "tenderfoot" who goes through the West "heeled," and ready to show that though he is from the effete East, he is able to take care of himself.

It was first brought home to me as I was returning from the border, where I had been with the troops who were hunting for Garza, and was waiting at a little station on the prairie to take the train for Corpus Christi. I was then told politely by a gentleman who seemed of authority, that if I did not take off that pistol I would be fined twenty-five dollars, or put in jail for twenty days. I explained to him where I had been, and that my baggage was at "Corpus," and that I had no other place to carry it. At which he apologized, and directed a deputy sheriff, who was also going to Corpus Christi, to see that I was not arrested for carrying a deadly weapon.

This, I think, illustrates a condition of things in darkest Texas which may give a new point of view to the Eastern mind. It is possibly something of a revelation to find that instead of every man protecting himself, and the selection of the fittest depending on who is "quickest on the trigger," he has to have an officer of the law to protect him if he tries to be a law unto himself.

While I was on the border a deputy sheriff named Rufus Glover, who was acting as a guide for Captain Chase, of the Third Cavalry, was fired upon from an ambush by persons unknown, and killed. A Mexican brought the news of this to our camp the night after the murder, and described the manner of the killing, as it had occurred, at great length and with much detail.

Except that he was terribly excited, and made a very dramatic picture as he stood in the fire-light and moonlight and acted the murder, it did not interest me, as I considered it to be an unfortunate event of very common occurrence in that part of the world. But the next morning every ranchman and cowboy and Texas Ranger and soldier we chanced to meet on the trail to Captain Hunter's camp took up the story of the murder of Rufus Glover, and told and retold what some one else had told him, with desperate earnestness and the most wearying reiteration. And on the day following, when the papers reached us, we found that reporters had been sent to the scene of the murder from almost every part of south-west Texas, many of whom had had to travel a hundred miles, and then ride thirty more through the brush before they reached it. How many city editors in New York City would send as far as that for anything less important than a railroad disaster or a Johnstown flood?

On the fourth day after the murder of this in no way celebrated or unusually popular individual, the people of Duval County, in which he had been killed, called an indignation meeting, and passed resolutions condemning the county officials for not suppressing crime, and petitioning

the Governor of the State to send the Rangers to put an
end to such lawlessness—that is, the killing of one man in
an almost uninhabited country. The committee who were
to present this petition passed through Laredo on the way
to see the Governor. Laredo is one hundred miles from
the scene of the murder, and in an entirely different county;
but there the popular indignation and excitement were so
great that another mass-meeting was called, and another
petition was made to the Governor, in which the resolutions
of Duval County were endorsed. I do not know what his
Excellency did about it. There were in the Tombs in New
York when I left that city twenty-five men awaiting trial
for murder, and that crime was so old a story in the Bend
and along the East Side that the most morbid newspaper
reader skipped the scant notice the papers gave of them.
It would seem from this that the East should reconstruct a
new Wild West for itself, in which a single murder sends
two committees of indignant citizens to the State capital
to ask the Governor what he intends to do about it.

But the West is not wholly reconstructed. There are
still the Texas Rangers, and in them the man from the
cities of the East will find the picturesqueness of the Wild
West show and its happiest expression. If they and the
sight of cowboys roping cattle do not satisfy him, nothing
else will. The Rangers are a semi-militia, semi-military organization of long descent, and with the most brilliant record of border warfare. At the present time their work is
less adventurous than it was in the day of Captain McNelly,
but the spirit of the first days has only increased with time.

The Rangers enlist for a year under one of eight captains, and the State pays them a dollar a day and supplies
them with rations and ammunition. They bring with them

their own horse, blanket, and rifle, and revolver; they wear no regular uniform or badge of any sort, except the belt of cartridges around the waist. The mounted police of the gold days in the Australian bush, and the mounted constabulary of the Canadian border are perhaps the only other organizations of a like nature and with similar duties. Their headquarters are wherever their captain finds water, and, if he is fortunate, fuel and shade; but as the latter two are difficult to find in common in the five hundred square miles of brush along the Rio Grande, they are content with a tank of alkali water alone.

There are about twenty men in each of the eight troops, and one or two of them are constantly riding away on detached service—to follow the trail of a Mexican bandit or a horse-thief, or to suppress a family feud. The Rangers' camps look much like those of gypsies, with their one wagon to carry the horses' feed, the ponies grazing at the ends of the lariats, the big Mexican saddles hung over the nearest barb fence, and the blankets covering the ground and marking the hard beds of the night before. These men are the especial pride of General Mabry, the Adjutant-general of Texas, who was with them the first time I met them, sharing their breakfast of bacon and coffee under the shade of the only tree within ten miles. He told me some very thrilling stories of their deeds and personal meetings with the desperadoes and "bad" men of the border; but when he tried to lead Captain Brooks into relating a few of his own adventures, the result was a significant and complete failure. Significant, because big men cannot tell of the big things they do as well as other people can—they are handicapped by having to leave out the best part; and because Captain Brooks's version of the same story the general had told me, with all the necessary detail, would be: "Well, we got word they were hiding in a ranch down in Zepata County, and we went down there and took 'em—which they were afterwards hung."

The fact that he had had three fingers shot off as he "took 'em" was a detail he scorned to remember, especially as he could shoot better without these members than the rest of his men, who had only lost one or two.

Boots above the knee and leather leggings, a belt three inches wide with two rows of brass-bound cartridges, and a slanting sombrero make a man appear larger than he really is; but the Rangers were the largest men I saw in Texas, the State of big men. And some of them were remarkably handsome in a sun-burned, broad-shouldered, easy, manly way. They were also somewhat shy with the strangers, listening very intently, but speaking little, and then in a slow, gentle voice; and as they spoke so seldom, they seemed to think what they had to say was too valuable to spoil by profanity.

When General Mabry found they would not tell of their adventures, he asked them to show how they could shoot; and as this was something they could do, and not something already done, they went about it as gleefully as schoolboys at recess doing "stunts." They placed a board, a foot wide and two feet high, some sixty feet off in the prairie, and Sheriff Scheeley opened hostilities by whipping out his revolver, turning it in the air, and shooting, with the sights upside down, into the bull's-eye of the impromptu target. He did this without discontinuing what he was saying to me, but rather as though he were punctuating his remarks with audible commas.

Then he said, "I didn't think you Rangers would let a

little one-penny sheriff get in the first shot on you." He could afford to say this, because he had been a Ranger himself, and his brother Joe was one of the best captains the Rangers have had; and he and all of his six brothers are over six feet high. But the taunt produced an instantaneous volley from every man in the company; they did not take the trouble to rise, but shot from where they happened to be sitting or lying and talking together, and the air rang with the reports and a hundred quick vibrating little gasps, like the singing of a wire string when it is tightened on a banjo.

They exhibited some most wonderful shooting. They shot with both hands at the same time, with the hammer underneath, holding the rifle in one hand, and never, when it was a revolver they were using, with a glance at the sights. They would sometimes fire four shots from a Winchester between the time they had picked it up from the ground and before it had nestled comfortably against their shoulder. They also sent one man on a pony racing around a tree about as thick as a man's leg, and were dissatisfied because he only put four out of six shots into it. Then General Mabry, who seemed to think I did not fully appreciate what they were doing, gave a Winchester rifle to Captain Brooks and myself, and told us to show which of us could first put eight shots into the target.

It seems that to shoot a Winchester you have to pull a trigger one way and work a lever backward and forward; this would naturally suggest that there are three movements —one to throw out the empty shell, one to replace it with another cartridge, and the third to explode this cartridge. Captain Brooks, as far as I could make out from the sound, used only one movement for his entire eight shots. As I guessed, the trial was more to show Captain Brooks's quickness rather than his marksmanship, and I paid no attention to the target, but devoted myself assiduously to manipulating the lever and trigger, aiming blankly at the prairie. When I had fired two shots into space, the captain had put his eight into the board. They sounded, as they went off, like fire-crackers well started in a barrel, and mine, in comparison, like minute-guns at sea. The Rangers, I found, after I saw more of them, could shoot as rapidly with a revolver as with a rifle, and had become so expert with the smaller weapon that instead of pressing the trigger for each shot, they would pull steadily on it, and snap the hammer until the six shots were exhausted.

San Antonio is the oldest of Texan cities, and possesses historical and picturesque show-places which in any other country but our own would be visited by innumerable American tourists prepared to fall down and worship. The citizens of San Antonio do not, as a rule, appreciate the historical values of their city; they are rather tired of them. They would prefer you should look at the new Post-office and the City Hall, and ride on the cable road. But the missions which lie just outside of the city are what will bring the Eastern man or woman to San Antonio, and not the new water-works. There are four of these missions, the two largest and most interesting being the Mission de la Conception, of which the corner-stone was laid in 1730, and the Mission San José, the carving, or what remains of it, in the latter being wonderfully rich and effective. The Spaniards were forced to abandon the missions on account of the hostility of the Indians, and they have been occupied at different times since by troops and bats, and left to the mercies of the young men from "Rochester, N. Y.," and the young women from "Dallas, Texas," who have carved their immortal names over their walls just as freely as though they were the pyramids of Egypt or Blarney Castle. San Antonio is a great place for invalids, on account of its moderate climate, and a most satisfactory place in which to spend a week or two in the winter whether one is an invalid or not. There is the third largest army post in the country at the edge of the city, where there is much to see and many interesting people to know, and there is a good club, and cock-fighting on Sunday, and a first-rate theatre all the week. At night the men sit outside of the hotels, and the plazas are filled with Mexicans and their open-air restaurants, and the lights of these and the brigandish appearance of those who keep them are very unlike anything one may see at home.

All that the city really needs now is a good hotel and a more proper pride in its history and the monuments to it. The man who seems to appreciate this best is William Corner, whose book on San Antonio is a most valuable historical authority.

A few years ago one would have said that San Antonio was enjoying a boom. But you cannot use that expression now, for the Western men have heard that a boom, no matter how quickly it rises, often comes down just as quickly, and so forcibly that it makes a hole in the ground where castles in the air had formerly stood. So if you wish to please a Western man by speaking well of his city (and you cannot please him more in any other way), you must say that it is enjoying a "steady, healthy growth." San Antonio is enjoying a steady, healthy growth.

It is quite as impossible to write comprehensively of south-western Texas in one article as it is to write such an article and say nothing of the Alamo. And the Alamo, in the event of any hasty reader's possible objection, is not ancient history. It is no more ancient history than love is an old story, for nothing is ancient and nothing is old which every new day teaches something that is fine and beautiful and brave. The Alamo is to the South-west what Independence Hall is to the United States, and Bunker Hill to the East; but the pride of it belongs to every American, whether he lives in Texas or in Maine. The battle of the Alamo was the event of greatest moment in the war between Mexico and the Texans, when Santa Anna was President, and the Texans were fighting for their independence. And the stone building to which the Mexicans laid siege, and in which the battle was fought, stands to-day facing a plaza in the centre of San Antonio.

There are hideous wooden structures around it, and others not so hideous—modern hotels and the new Post-office, on which the mortar is hardly yet dry. But in spite of these the grace and dignity which the monks gave it in 1774, raise it above these modern efforts that tower above it, and dwarf them. They are collecting somewhat slowly a fund to pay for the erection of a monument to the heroes of the Alamo. As though they needed a monument, with these battered walls still standing and the marks of the bullets on the casements! No architect can build better than that. No architect can introduce that feature. The architects of the Alamo were building the independence of a State as wide in its boundaries as the German Empire.

The story of the Alamo is a more than thrice-told one, and Sidney Lanier has told it so well that whoever would write of it must draw on him for much of their material, and must accept his point of view. But it cannot be told too often, even though it is spoiled in the telling.

On the 23d of February, 1836, General Santa Anna himself, with four thousand Mexican soldiers, marched into the town of San Antonio. In the old mission of the Alamo were the town's only defenders, one hundred and forty-five men, under Captain Travis, a young man twenty-eight years old. With him were Davy Crockett, who had crossed over from his own State to help those who were freeing theirs, and Colonel Bowie (who gave his name to a knife, which name our government gave later to a fort), who was wounded and lying on a cot.

Their fortress and quarters and magazine was the mission, their artillery fourteen mounted pieces, but there was little ammunition. Santa Anna demanded unconditional surrender, and the answer was ten days of dogged defence, and skirmishes by day and sorties for food and water by night. The Mexicans lost heavily during the first days of the siege, but not one inside of the Alamo was killed. Early in the week Travis had despatched couriers for help, and the defenders of the mission were living in the hope of re-enforcements; but four days passed, and neither couriers returned nor re-enforcements came. On the fourth day Colonel Fannin with three hundred men and four pieces of artillery started forth from Goliad, but put back again for want of food and lack of teams. The garrison of the Alamo never knew of this. On the 1st of March Captain John W. Smith, who *has* found teams, and who *has* found rations, brings an offering of thirty-two men from Gonzales, and leads them safely into the fort. They have come with forced marches to their own graves; but they do not know that, and the garrison, now one hundred and seventy-two

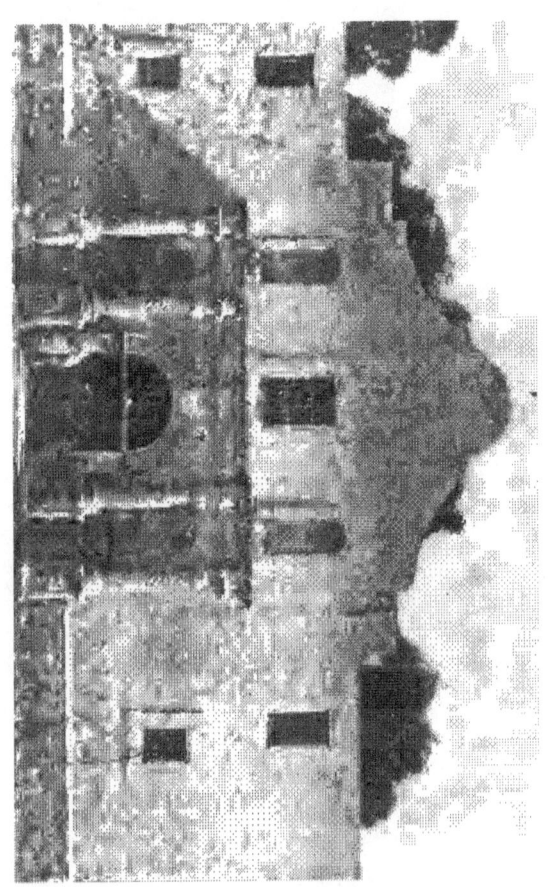

strong, against four thousand Mexicans, continues its desperate sorties and its desperate defence.

On the 3d of March, 1836, there is a cessation in the bombardment, and Captain Travis draws his men up into single rank and takes his place in front of them.

He tells them that he has deceived them with hopes of re-enforcements—false hopes based on false promises of help from the outside—but he does not blame those who failed him; he makes excuses for them; they have tried to reach him, no doubt, but have been killed on the way. Sidney Lanier quotes this excusing of those who had deserted him at the very threshold of death as best showing the fineness of Travis, and the poet who has judged the soldier so truly has touched here one of the strongest points of this story of great heroism.

Captain Travis tells them that all that remains to them is the choice of their death, and that they have but to decide in which manner of dying they will best serve their country. They can surrender and be shot down mercilessly, they can make a sortie and be butchered before they have gained twenty yards, or they can die fighting to the last, and killing their enemies until that last comes.

He gives them their choice, and then stooping, draws a line with the point of his sword in the ground from the left to the right of the rank.

"And now," he says, "every man who is determined to remain here and to die with me will come to me across that line."

Tapley Holland was the first to cross. He jumped it with a bound, as though it were a Rubicon. "I am ready to die for my country," he said.

And then all but one man, named Rose, marched over to

the other side. Colonel Bowie, lying wounded in his cot, raised himself on his elbow. "Boys," he said, "don't leave me. Won't some of you carry me across?"

And those of the sick who could walk rose from the bunks and tottered across the line; and those who could not walk were carried. Rose, who could speak Spanish, trusted to this chance to escape, and scaling the wall of the Alamo, dropped into a ditch on the other side, and crawled, hidden by the cactus, into a place of safety. Through him we know what happened before that final day came. He had his reward.

Three days after this, on the morning of the 6th of March, Santa Anna brought forward all of his infantry, supported by his cavalry, and stormed the fortress. The infantry came up on every side at once in long, black solid rows, bearing the scaling-ladders before them, and encouraged by the press of great numbers about them.

But the band inside the mission drove them back, and those who held the ladders dropped them on the ground and ran against the bayonets of their comrades. A second time they charged into the line of bullets, and the second time they fell back, leaving as many dead at the foot of the ladders as there were standing at bay within the walls. But at the third trial the ladders are planted, and Mexicans after Mexicans scale them, and jump down into the pit inside, hundreds and hundreds of them, to be met with bullets and then by bayonet-thrusts, and at last with desperate swinging of the butt, until the little band grows smaller and weaker, and is driven up and about and beaten down and stamped beneath the weight of overwhelming and unending numbers. They die fighting on their knees, hacking up desperately as they are beaten and pinned down by a dozen bayonets, Bowie leaning on his elbow and shooting from his cot, Crockett fighting like a panther in the angle of the church wall, and Travis with his back against the wall to the west. The one hundred and seventy-two men who had held four thousand men at bay for two sleepless weeks are swept away as a dam goes that has held back a flood, and the Mexicans open the church doors from the inside and let in their comrades and the sunshine that shows them horrid heaps of five hundred and twenty-two dead Mexicans, and five hundred more wounded.

There are no wounded among the Texans; of the one hundred and seventy-two who were in the Alamo there are one hundred and seventy-two dead.

With an example like this to follow, it was not difficult to gain the independence of Texas; and whenever Sam Houston rode before his men, crying, "Remember the Alamo!" the battle was already half won.

It was not a cry wholly of revenge, I like to think. It was rather the holding up of the cross to the crusaders, and crying, "By this sign we conquer." It was a watchword to remind men of those who had suffered and died that their cause might live.

And so, when we leave Texas, we forget the little things that may have tried our patience and understanding there, we forgive the desolation of the South-west, its cactus and dying cattle, we forget the dinners in the middle of the day and the people's passing taste in literature, and we remember the Alamo.

II

OUR TROOPS ON THE BORDER

II

OUR TROOPS ON THE BORDER

A ROLLING, jerky train made up of several freight and one passenger car, the latter equally divided, "For Whites" and "For Negroes" —which in the south-west of Texas reads "Mexicans"—dropped my baggage at Pena station, and rolled off across the prairie, rocking from side to side like a line of canal-boats in a rough sea. It seemed like the last departing link of civilization. There was the freight station itself; beyond the track a leaky water-tank, a wooden store surrounded with piles of raw, foul-smelling hides left in exchange for tobacco and meal, a few thatched Mexican huts, and the prairie. That stretched on every side to the horizon, level and desolate, and rising and falling in the heat. Beneath was a red sandy soil covered with cactus and bunches of gray, leafless brush, marked with the white skeletons of cattle, and overhead a sun at white heat, and heavily moving buzzards wheeling in circles or balancing themselves with outstretched wings between the hot sky above and the hot, red soil below.

Across this desert came slowly Trumpeter Tyler, of Troop G, Third Cavalry, mounted on the white horse which only trumpeters affect, and as white as the horse itself from the dust of the trail. He did not look like the soldiers I had seen at San Antonio. His blue shirt was wide open at the breast, his riding-breeches were bare at the knee, and the cactus and chaparral had torn his blouse into rags and ribbons. He pushed his wide-brimmed hat back from his forehead and breathed heavily with the heat. Captain Hardie's camp, he panted, lay twenty-five miles to the west. He had come from there to see if the field tents and extra rations were ever going to arrive from the post, and as he had left, the captain had departed also with a detachment in search of Garza on a fresh trail. "And he means to follow it," said Trumpeter Tyler, "if it takes him into Mexico." So it was doubtful whether the visitor from the East would see the troop commander for several days; but if he nevertheless wished to push on to the camp, Trumpeter Tyler would be glad to show him the way. Not only would he show him the way, but he would look over his kit for him, and select such things as the visitor would need in the brush. Not such things as the visitor might want, but such things as the visitor would need. For in the brush necessities become luxuries, and luxuries are relics of an effete past and of places where tradition tells of pure water and changes of raiment, and, some say, even beds. Neither Trumpeter Tyler, nor Captain Francis H. Hardie, nor any of the officers or men of the eight troops of cavalry on field service in south-west Texas had seen such things for three long months of heat by day and cold by night, besides a blizzard of sleet and rain, that kept them trembling with cold for a fortnight. And it was for this reason that the visitor from the East chose to see the United States troops as they were in the field, and to tell about the way they performed their duty there, rather than as he found them at the posts, where there is

TRUMPETER TYLER

at least a canteen and papers not more than a week old.

Trumpeter Tyler ran his hand haughtily through what I considered a very sensibly-chosen assortment of indispensable things, and selected a handful which he placed on one side.

"You think I had better not take those?" I suggested.

"That's all you can take," said the trooper, mercilessly. "You must think of the horse."

Then he led the way to the store, and pointed out the value of a tin plate, a tin cup, and an iron knife and fork, saddle-bags, leather leggings to keep off the needles of the cactus, a revolver, and a blanket. It is of interest to give Trumpeter Tyler's own outfit, as it was that of every other man in the troop, and was all that any one of them had had for two months. He carried it all on his horse, and it consisted of a blanket, an overcoat, a carbine, a feed-bag, lariat and iron stake, a canteen, saddle-bags filled with rations on one side and a change of under-clothing on the other, a shelter-tent done up in a roll, a sword, and a revolver, with rounds of ammunition for it and the carbine worn in a belt around the waist. All of this, with the saddle, weighed about eighty pounds, and when the weight of a man is added to it, one can see that it is well, as Trumpeter Tyler suggested, to think of the horse. Troop G had been ordered out for seven days' field service on the 15th of December, and it was then the 24th of January, and the clothes and equipments they had had with them when they started at midnight from Fort MacIntosh for that week of hard riding were all they had had with them since. But the hard riding had continued.

Trumpeter Tyler proved that day not only my guide, but a philosopher, and when night came on, a friend. He was very young, and came from Virginia, as his slow, lazy voice showed; and he had played, in his twenty-three years, the many parts of photographer, compositor, barber, cook, musician, and soldier. He talked of these different callings as we walked our horses over the prairie, and, out of deference to myself and my errand, of writing. He was a somewhat general reader, and volunteered his opinion of the works of Rudyard Kipling, Laura Jean Libbey, Captain Charles King, and others with confident familiarity. He recognized no distinctions in literature; they had all written a book, therefore they were, in consequence, in exactly the same class.

Of Mr. Kipling he said, with an appreciative shake of the head, that "he knew the private soldier from way back;" of Captain Charles King, that he wrote for the officers; and of Laura Jean Libbey, that she was an authoress whose books he read "when there really wasn't nothing else to do." I doubt if one of Mr. Kipling's own heroes could have made as able criticisms.

When night came on and the stars came out, he dropped the soldier shop and talked of religion and astronomy. The former, he assured me earnestly, was much discussed by the privates around the fire at night, which I could better believe after I saw how near the stars get and how wide the world seems when there is only a blanket between you and the heavens, and when there is a general impression prevailing that you are to be shot at from an ambush in the morning. Of astronomy he showed a very wonderful knowledge, and awakened my admiration by calling many stars by strange and ancient names—an admiration which was lessened abruptly when he confessed that he had been following some other than the North Star for the last three miles, and that we were lost. It was a warm night, and I was so tired with the twenty-five-miles ride on a Mexican saddle—which is as comfortable as a soap-box turned edges up—that the idea of lying out on the ground did not alarm me. But Trumpeter Tyler's honor was at stake. He had his reputation as a trailer to maintain, and he did so ably by lighting matches and gazing knowingly at the hoof-marks of numerous cattle, whose bones, I was sure, were already whitening on the plain or journeying East in a refrigerator-car, but which he assured me were still fresh, and must lead to the ranch near which the camp was pitched. And so, after four hours' aimless trailing through the chaparral, when only the thorns of the cactus kept us from falling asleep off our horses, we stumbled into two smouldering fires, a ghostly row of little shelter-tents, and a tall figure in a long overcoat, who clicked a carbine and cried, "Halt, and dismount!"

I was somewhat doubtful of my reception in the absence of the captain, and waited, very wide awake now, while they consulted together in whispers, and then the sentry led me to one of the little tents and kicked a sleeping form violently, and told me to crawl in and not to mind reveille in the morning, but to sleep on as long as I wished. I did not know then that I had Trumpeter Tyler's bed, and that he was sleeping under a wagon, but I was gratefully conscious of his "bunkie's" tucking me in as tenderly as though I were his son, and of his not sharing, but giving me more than my share of the blankets. And I went to sleep so quickly that it was not until the morning that I found what I had drowsily concluded must be the roots of trees under me, to be "bunkie's" sabre and carbine.

The American private, as he showed himself during the

three days in which I was his guest, and afterwards, when Captain Hardie had returned and we went scouting together, proved to be a most intelligent and unpicturesque individual. He was intelligent, because he had, as a rule, followed some other calling before he entered the service, and he was not picturesque, because he looked on "soldiering" merely as a means of livelihood, and had little or no patriotic or sentimental feeling concerning it. This latter was not true of the older men. They had seen real war either during the rebellion or in the Indian campaigns, which are much more desperate affairs than the Eastern mind appreciates, and they were fond of the service and proud of it. One of the corporals in G Troop, for instance, had been honorably discharged a year before with the rank of first sergeant, and had re-enlisted as a private rather than give up the service, of which he found he was more fond than he had imagined when he had left it. And in K Troop was an even more notable instance in a man who had been retired on three-fourths pay, having served his thirty years, and who had returned to the troop to act as Captain Hunter's "striker," or man of all work, and who bore the monotony of the barracks and the hardships of field service rather than lose the uniform and the feeling of *esprit de corps* which thirty years' service had made a necessity to him.

But the raw recruit, or the man in his third or fourth year, as he expressed himself in the different army posts and among the companies I met on the field, looked upon his work from a purely business point of view. He had been before enlistment a clerk, or a compositor, a cowboy, a day-laborer, painter, blacksmith, book-canvasser, almost everything. In Captain Hardie's troop all of these were represented, and the average of intelligence was very high. Whether the most intelligent private is the best soldier is a much-discussed question which is not to be discussed here, but these men were intelligent and were good soldiers, although I am sure they were too independent in their thoughts, though not in their actions, to have suited an officer of the English or German army. That they are more carefully picked men than those found in the rank and file of the British army can be proved from the fact that of those who apply for enlistment in the United States but twenty per cent. are chosen, while in Great Britain they accept eighty and in some years ninety per cent. of the applicants. The small size of our army in comparison, however, makes this showing less favorable than it at first appears.

In camp, while the captain was away, the privates suggested a lot of college boys more than any other body of individuals. A few had the college boy's delight in shirking their work, and would rejoice over having had a dirty carbine pass inspection on account of a shining barrel, as the Sophomore boasts of having gained a high marking for a translation he had read from a crib. They had also the college boy's songs, and his trick of giving nicknames, and his original and sometimes clever slang, and his satisfaction in expressing violent liking or dislike for those in authority over him—in the one case tutors and professors, and in the other sergeants and captains. Their one stupid hitch, in which the officers shared to some extent, was in re-enforcing all they said with profanity; but as soldiers have done this, apparently, since the time of Shakespeare's Seven Ages, it must be considered an inherited characteristic. Their fun around the camp fire at night was rough, but it was sometimes clever, though it was open to the objection that a clever story never failed of three or four repetitions. The greatest successes were those in which the officers, always of some other troop, were the butts. One impudent "cruitie" made himself famous in a night by improvising an interview between himself and a troop commander who had met him that day as he was steering a mule train across the prairie.

"'How are you?' said he to me. 'You're one of Captain Hardie's men, ain't you? I'm Captain——.'

"'Glad to know you, captain,' said I. 'I've read about you in the papers.'"

This was considered a magnificent stroke by the men, who thought the captain in question rather too fond of sending in reports concerning himself to headquarters.

"'Well,' says he, 'when do you think we're going to catch this —— —— —— —— Garza? As for me,' says he, 'I'm that —— —— —— —— tired of the whole —— —— —— business that I'm willing to give up my job to any —— —— —— fool that will take it ——.'

"'Well, old man,' says I, 'I'd be glad to relieve you,' says I, 'but I'd a —— sight rather serve under Captain Hardie than captain such a lot of regular —— —— —— coffee-coolers as you've got under you.'"

The audacity of this entirely fictitious conversation was what recommended it to the men. I only reproduce it here as showing their idea of humor. An even greater success was that of a stolid German, who related a true incident of life at Fort Clarke, where the men were singing one night, around the fire, when the colonel passed by, and ordered them into the tents, and to stop that —— noise.

"And den," continued the soldier, "he come acrost Cab-

CAPTAIN FRANCIS H. HARDIE, G TROOP, THIRD UNITED STATES CAVALRY

ding ——, sitting in frond of his tent, and he says to him quick like that, 'You ged into your tent, *too*.' That's what he said to him, 'You ged into your tent, *too*.'"

It is impossible to imagine the exquisite delight that this simple narrative gave. The idea of a real troop commander having been told to get into his tent just like a common soldier brought the tears to the men's eyes, and the success of his story so turned the German's head that he continued repeating to himself and to any one he met for several days: "That's what he said, 'You ged into your tent, TOO.' That's what he said."

Captain Hardie rode his detachment into camp on the third day, with horses so tired that they tried to lie down whenever there was a halt; and a horse must be very tired before he will do that. Captain Hardie's riding-breeches were held together by the yellow stripes at their sides, and his hands were raw and swollen with the marks of the cactus needles, and his face burned and seared to a dull red. I had heard of him through the papers and from the officers at headquarters as the "Riding Captain," and as the one who had during the Garza campaign been most frequently in the saddle, and least given to sending in detailed reports of his own actions. He had been absolutely alone for the two months he had been in the field. He was the father of his men, as all troop commanders must be; he had to doctor them when they were ill, to lend them money when the paymaster lost his way in the brush, to write their letters, and to listen to their grievances, and explain that it was not because they were not good soldiers that they could not go out and risk being shot on this or that particular scouting party—he could do all this for them, but he could not talk to them. He had to sit in front of his own camp fire and

The West from a Car-Window

hear them laughing around theirs, and consider the loneliness of south-western Texas, which is the loneliness of the ocean at night. He could talk to his Mexican guides, because they, while they were under him, were not of his troop, and I believe it was this need to speak to some living soul that taught Captain Hardie to know Spanish as well as he did, and much more quickly than the best of tutors could have done in a year at the post.

The Eastern mind does not occupy itself much with these guardians of its borders ; its idea of the soldier is the comfortable, clubable fellow they meet in Washington and New York, whose red, white, and blue button is all that marks him from the other clubable, likable men about him. But they ought to know more and feel more for these equally likable men of the border posts, whose only knowledge of club life is the annual bill for dues, one of which, with supreme irony, arrived in Captain Hardie's mail at a time when we had only bacon three times a day, and nothing but alkali water to silence the thirst that followed. To a young man it is rather pathetic to see another young man, with a taste and fondness for the pleasant things of this world, pull out his watch and hold it to the camp fire and say, "Just seven o'clock ; people in God's country are sitting down to dinner." And then a little later : "And now it's eight o'clock, and they are going to the theatres. What is there at the theatres now ?" And when I recalled the plays running in New York when I left it, the officers would select which one they would go to, with much grave deliberation, and then crawl in between two blankets and find the most comfortable angle at which a McClellan saddle will make a pillow.

The Garza campaign is only of interest here as it shows

Our Troops on the Border

the work of the United States troops who were engaged in it. As for Caterino E. Garza himself, he may, by the time this appears in print, have been made President of Mexico, which is most improbable; or have been captured in the brush, which is more improbable; or he may have disappeared from public notice altogether. It is only of interest to the Eastern man to know that a Mexican ranch-owner and sometime desperado and politician living in south-west Texas proclaimed a revolution against the Government of Mexico, and that that Government requested ours to see that the neutrality laws existing between the two countries were not broken by the raising of troops on our side of the Rio Grande River, and that followers of this Garcia should not be allowed to cross through Texas on their way to Mexico. This our Government, as represented by the Department of Texas, which has its headquarters at San Antonio, showed its willingness to do by sending at first two troops of cavalry, and later six more, into darkest Texas, with orders to take prisoners any bands of revolutionists they might find there; and to arrest all individual revolutionists with a warrant sworn to by two witnesses. The country into which these eight troops were sent stretches for three hundred and sixty miles along the Rio Grande River, where it separates Mexico from Texas, and runs back a hundred and more miles east, making of this so-called Garza territory an area of five hundred square miles.

This particular country is the back-yard of the world. It is to the rest of the West what the ash-covered lots near High Bridge are to New York. It is the country which led General Sheridan to say that if he owned both places, he would rent Texas and live in hell. It is the strip of country over which we actually went to war with Mexico, and which gave General Sherman the opportunity of making the epigramme, which no one who has not seen the utter desolateness of the land can justly value, that we should go to war with Mexico again, and force her to take it back.

It is a country where there are no roses, but where everything that grows has a thorn. Where the cattle die of starvation, and where the troops had to hold up the solitary train that passes over it once a day, in true road-agent fashion, to take the water from its boilers that their horses might not drop for lack of it. It is a country where the sun blinds and scorches at noon, and where the dew falls like a cold rain at night, and where one shivers in an overcoat at breakfast, and rides without coat or waistcoat and panting with the heat the same afternoon. Where there are no trees, nor running streams, nor rocks nor hills, but just an ocean of gray chaparral and white, chalky cañons or red, dusty trails. If you leave this trail for fifty yards, you may wander for twenty miles before you come to water or a ranch or another trail, and by that time the chaparral and cactus will have robbed you of your clothing, and left in its place a covering of needles, which break when one attempts to draw them out, and remain in the flesh to fester and swell the skin, and leave it raw and tender for a week. This country, it is almost a pleasure to say, is America's only in its possession. No white men, or so few that they are not as common as century-plants, live in it. It is Mexican in its people, its language, and its mode of life. The few who inhabit its wilderness are ranch-owners, and their shepherds and cowboys; and a ranch, which means a store and six or seven thatched adobe houses around it, is at the nearest three miles from the next ranch, and on an average

WATER

twenty miles. As a rule, they move farther away the longer you ride towards them.

Into this foreign country of five hundred square miles the eight United States cavalry troops of forty men each and two companies of infantry were sent to find Garza and his followers. The only means by which a man or horses or cows can be tracked in this desert is by the foot or hoof prints which they may leave in the sandy soil as they follow the trails already made or make fresh ones. To follow these trails it is necessary to have as a guide a man born in the brush, who has trailed cattle for a livelihood. The Mexican Government supplied the troops with some of their own people, who did not know the particular country into which they were sent, but who could follow a trail in any country. One or two of these, sometimes none, went with each troop. What our Government should have done was to supply each troop commander with five or six of these men, who could have gone out in search of trails, and reported at the camp whenever they had found a fresh one. By this means the troops could have been saved hundreds of miles of unnecessary marching and countermarching on "false alarms," and the Government much money, as the campaign in that event would have been brought much more rapidly to a conclusion.

But the troop commanders in the field had no such aids. They had to ride forth whenever so ordered to do by the authorities at headquarters, some two hundred miles from the scene of the action, who had in turn received their information from the Mexican general on the other side of the Rio Grande. This is what made doing their duty, as represented by obeying orders, such a difficult thing to the troops in the Garza territory. They knew before they saddled their horses that they were going out on a wild-goose chase to wear out their horses and their own patience, and to accomplish nothing beyond furnishing Garza's followers with certain satisfaction in seeing a large body of men riding solemnly through a dense underbrush in a blinding sun to find a trail which a Mexican general had told an American general would be sure to lead them to Garza, and news of which had reached them a week after whoever had made the trail had passed over it. They could imagine, as they trotted in a long, dusty line through the chaparral, as conspicuous marks on the plain as a prairie-wagon, that Garza or his men were watching them from under a clump of cactus on some elevation in the desert, and that he would say:

"Ah! the troops are out again, I see. Who is it to-day—Hardie, Chase, or Hunter? Lend me your field-glass. Ah! it is Hardie. He is a good rider. I hope he will not get a sunstroke."

And then they would picture how the revolutionists would continue the smoking of their cornstalk cigarettes and the drinking of the smuggled muscal.

This is not an exaggerated picture. A man could lie hidden in this brush and watch the country on every side of him, and see each of the few living objects which might pass over it in a day, as easily as he could note the approach of a three-masted schooner at sea. And even though troops came directly towards him, he had but to lie flat in the brush within twenty feet of them, and they would not know it. It would be as easy to catch Jack the Ripper with a Lord-Mayor's procession as Garza with a detachment of cavalry, unless they stumbled upon him by luck, or unless he had with him so many men that their trail could be followed at a gallop. As a matter of fact and history, the Garza movement was broken up in the first three weeks of its inception by the cavalry and the Texas Rangers and the deputy sheriffs, who rode after the large bodies of men and scattered them. After that it was merely a chase after little bands of from three to a dozen men, who travelled by night and slept by day in their race towards the river, or, when met there by the Mexican soldiers, in their race back again. The fact that every inhabitant of the ranches and every Mexican the troops met was a secret sympathizer with Garza was another and most important difficulty in the way of his pursuers. And it was trying to know that the barking of the dogs of a ranch was not yet out of ear-shot before a *vaquero* was scuttling off through the chaparral to tell the hiding revolutionists that the troops were on their way, and which way they were coming.

And so, while it is no credit to soldiers to do their duty, it is creditable to them when they do their duty knowing that it is futile, and that some one has blundered. If a fire company in New York City were ordered out on a false alarm every day for three months, knowing that it was not a fire to which they were going, but that some one had wanted a messenger-boy, and rung up an engine by mistake, the alertness and fidelity of those firemen would be most severely tested. That is why I admired, and why the readers in the East should admire, the discipline and the faithfulness with which the cavalry on the border of Texas did their duty the last time Trumpeter Tyler sounded "Boots and Saddles," and went forth as carefully equipped, and as eager and hopeful that *this* time meant fighting, as they did the first.

The West from a Car-Window

Their life in the field was as near to nature, and, as far as comforts were concerned, to the beasts of the field, as men often come. A tramp in the Eastern States lives like a respectable householder in comparison. Suppose, to better understand it, that you were ordered to leave your house or flat or hall bedroom and live in the open air for two months, and that you were limited in your selection of what you wished to carry with you to the weight of eighty pounds. You would find it difficult to adjust this eighty pounds in such a way that it would include any comforts; certainly, there would be no luxuries. The soldiers of Troop G, besides the things before enumerated, were given for a day's rations a piece of bacon as large as your hand, as much coffee as would fill three large cups, and enough flour to make five or six heavy biscuits, which they justly called "'dobes," after the clay bricks of which Mexican adobe houses are made. In camp they received potatoes and beans. All of these things were of excellent quality and were quite satisfying, as the work supplies an appetite to meet them. This is not furnished by the Government, and costs it nothing, but it is about the best article in the line of sustenance that the soldier receives. He sleeps on a blanket with his "bunkie," and with his "bunkie's" blanket over him. If he is cold, he can build the fire higher, and doze in front of that. He rides, as a rule, from seven in the morning to five in the afternoon, without a halt for a noonday meal, and he generally gets to sleep by eight or nine. The rest of the time he is in the saddle. Each man carries a frying-pan about as large as a plate, with an iron handle, which folds over and is locked in between the pan and another iron plate that closes upon it. He does his own cooking in this, unless he happens to be the captain's "striker," when he has

"THE MEXICAN GUIDE"

double duty. He is so equipped and so taught that he is an entirely independent organization in himself, and he and his horse eat and sleep and work as a unit, and are as much and as little to the rest of the troop as one musket and bayonet are to the line of them when a company salutes.

We had for a guide one of the most picturesque ruffians I ever met. He was a Mexican murderer to the third or fourth degree, as Captain Hardie explained when I first met him, and had been liberated from a jail in Mexico in order that he might serve his country on this side of the river as a guide, and that his wonderful powers as a trailer might not be wasted.

He rejoiced in his liberty from iron bars and a bare mud floor, and showed his gratitude in the most untiring vigilance and in the endurance of what seemed to the Eastern mind the greatest discomforts. He always rode in advance of the column, and with his eyes wandering from the trail to the horizon and towards the backs of distant moving cattle, and again to the trail at his feet. Whenever he saw any one—and he could discover a suspected revolutionist long before any one else—the first intimation the rest of the scouting party would get of it was his pulling out his Winchester and disappearing on a gallop into the chaparral. He scorned the assistance of the troop, and when we came up to him again, after a wild dash through the brush, which left our hats and portions of our clothing to mark our way, we would find him with his prisoner's carbine tucked under his arm, and beaming upon him with a smile of wicked satisfaction.

As a trailer he showed, as do many of these guides, what seemed to be a gift of second-sight cultivated to a supernatural degree. He would say: "Five horses have passed ahead of us about an hour since. Two are led and one has two men on his back, and there is one on each of the other two;" which, when we caught up to them at the first watering-place, would prove to be true. Or he would tell us that troops or Rangers to such a number had crossed the trail at some time three or four days before, that a certain mark was made by a horse wandering without a rider, or that another had been made by a pony so many years old— all of which statements would be verified later. But it was as a would-be belligerent that he shone most picturesquely. When he saw a thin column of smoke rising from a cañon where revolutionists were supposed to be in camp, or came upon several armed men riding towards us and too close to escape, his face would light up with a smile of the most wicked content and delight, and he would beam like a cannibal before a feast as he pumped out the empty cartridges and murmured, "Buena! buena! buena!" with rolling eyes and an anticipatory smack of the lips.

But he was generally disappointed; the smoke would come from a shepherd's fire, and the revolutionists would point to the antelope-skins under their saddles, which had been several months in drying, and swear they were hunters, and call upon the saints to prove that they had never heard of such a man as Garza, and that carbines, revolvers, and knives were what every antelope-hunter needed for self-protection. At which the Mexican would show his teeth and roll his eyes with such a cruel show of disbelief that they would beg the "good captain" to protect them and let them go, which, owing to the fact that one cannot get a warrant and a notary public in the brush, as the regulations require, he would, after searching them, be compelled to do.

Our Troops on the Border

And then the Mexican, who had expected to see them hung to a tree until they talked or died, as would have been done in his own free republic, would sigh bitterly, and trot

THIRD CAVALRY TROOPERS — SEARCHING A SUSPECTED REVOLUTIONIST

off patiently and hopefully after more. Hope was especially invented for soldiers and fishermen. One thought of this when one saw the spirit of the men as they stole out at night, holding up their horses' heads to make them step lightly, and dodging the lights of the occasional ranches, and startling some shepherd sleeping by the trail into the belief that a file

of ghosts had passed by him in the mist. They were always
sure that this time it meant something, and if the captain
made a dash from the trail, and pounded with his fist on
the door of a ranch where lights shone when lights should
have been put out, the file of ghosts that had stretched back
two hundred yards into the night in an instant became a
close-encircling line of eager, open-eyed boys, with carbines
free from the sling-belts, covering the windows and the
grudgingly opened door. They never grew weary; they
rode on many days from nine at night to five the next afternoon, with but three hours' sleep. On one scouting expedition Tyler and myself rode one hundred and ten miles
in thirty-three hours; the average, however, was from thirty to fifty miles a day; but the hot, tired eyes of the enlisted men kept wandering over the burning prairie as
though looking for gold; and if on the ocean of cactus
they saw a white object move, or a sombrero drop from
sight, or a horse with a saddle on its back, they would
pass the word forward on the instant, and wait breathless-
ly until the captain saw it too.

I asked some of them what they thought of when they
were riding up to these wandering bands of revolutionists,
and they told me that from the moment the captain had
shouted "Howmp!" which is the only order he gives for
any and every movement, they had made themselves corporals, had been awarded the medal of honor, and had
spent the thirty thousand dollar reward for Garza's capture.
And so if any one is to take Garza, and the hunting of the
Snark is to be long continued in Texas, I hope it will be
G Troop, Third Cavalry, that brings the troublesome little
wretch into camp; not because they have worked so much
harder than the others, but because they had no tents, as

did the others, and no tinned goods, and no pay for two months, and because they had such an abundance of enthusiasm and hope, and the good cheer that does not come from the commissariat department or the canteen.

III

AT A NEW MINING CAMP

At a New Mining Camp

III

AT A NEW MINING CAMP

MY only ideas of a new mining camp before I visited Creede were derived from an early and eager study of Bret Harte. Not that I expected to see one of his mining camps or his own people when I visited Creede, but the few ideas of miners and their ways and manners that I had were those which he had given me. I should have liked, although I did not expect it, to see the outcasts of Poker Flat before John Oakhurst, in his well-fitting frock-coat, had left the outfit, and Yuba Bill pulling up his horses in front of the Lone Star saloon, where Colonel Starbuckle, with one elbow resting on the bar, and with his high white hat tipped to one side, waited to do him honor. I do not know that Bret Harte ever said that Colonel Starbuckle had a white hat, but I always pictured him in it, and with a black stock. I wanted to hear people say, " Waal, stranger," and to see auburn-haired giants in red shirts, with bags of gold-dust and nuggets of silver, and much should I have liked to meet Rose of Touloumme. But all that I found at Creede which reminded me of these miners and gamblers and the chivalric extravagant days of '49 were a steel pan, like a frying-pan without a handle, which I recognized with a thrill as the pan for washing gold, and a pick in the corner of a cabin; and once when a man hailed me as "Pardner" on the mountain-side, and asked "What luck?" The men and the scenes in this new silver camp showed what might have existed in the more glorious sunshine of California, but they were dim and commonplace, and lacked the sharp, clear-cut personality of Bret Harte's men and scenes. They were like the negative of a photo-

MINING CAMP ON THE RANGE ABOVE CREEDE

graph which has been under-exposed, and which no amount of touching up will make clear. So I will not attempt to touch them up.

When I first read of Creede, when I was so ignorant concerning it that I pronounced the final *e*, it was on the date line of a newspaper, and made no more impression upon me then than though it were printed simply *Creede*. But after I had reached Denver, and even before, when I had begun to find my way about the Western newspapers, it seemed to be spelled CREEDE. In Denver it faced you

At a New Mining Camp

everywhere from bill-boards, flaunted at you from canvas awnings stretched across the streets, and stared at you from daily papers in type an inch long; the shop-windows, according to their several uses, advertised "Photographs of Creede," "The only correct map of Creede," "Specimen ore from the Holy Moses Mine, Creede," "Only direct route to Creede," "Scalp tickets to Creede," "Wanted, $500 to start drug-store in Creede," "You will need boots at Creede, and you can get them at ——'s." The gentlemen in the Denver Club talk Creede; the people in the hotels dropped the word so frequently that you wondered if they were not all just going there, or were not about to write Creede on the register. It was a common language, starting-point, and interest. It was as momentous as the word Johnstown during the week after the flood.

The train which carried me there held stern, important-looking old gentlemen, who, the porter told me in an awed whisper, were one-third or one-fifteenth owners of the Potluck Mine; young men in Astrakhan fur coats and new top boots laced at the ankles, trying to look desperate and rough; grub-stake prospectors, with bedding, pick, and rations in a roll on the seat beside them; more young men, who naïvely assured me when they found that I, too, was going to Creede, and not in top-boots and revolvers and a flannel shirt, that they had never worn such things before, and really had decent clothes at home; also women who smoked with the men and passed their flasks down the length of the car, and two friendless little girls, of whom every one except the women, who seemed to recognize a certain fitness of things, took unremitting care. Every one on the crowded train showed the effect of the magnet that was drawing him—he was restless, impatient, and excited.

The West from a Car-Window

Half of them did not know what they were going to find; and the other half, who had already taken such another journey to Leadville, Aspen, or Cripple Creek, knew only too well, and yet hoped that *this* time—

Creede lies in a gully between two great mountains. In the summer the mountain streams wash down into this gully and turn it into a little river; but with the recklessness of true gamblers, the people who came to Creede built their stores, houses, and saloons as near the base of the great sides of the valley as they could, and if the stream comes next summer, as it has done for hundreds of years before, it will carry with it fresh pine houses and log huts instead of twigs and branches.

The train stopped at the opening of this gully, and its passengers jumped out into two feet of mud and snow. The ticket and telegraph office on one side of the track were situated in a freight car with windows and doors cut out of it, and with the familiar blue and white sign of the Western Union nailed to one end; that station was typical of the whole town in its rawness, and in the temporary and impromptu air of its inhabitants. If you looked back at the road over which you had just come, you saw the beautiful circle of the Wagon Wheel Gap, a chain of magnificent mountains white with snow, picked with hundreds of thousands of pine-trees so high above one that they looked like little black pins. The clouds, less white than the snow, lay packed in between the peaks of the range, or drifted from one to another to find a resting-place, and the sun, beating down on both a blinding glare, showed other mountains and other snow-capped ranges for fifty miles beyond. This is at the opening of Willow Gulch into which Creede has hurried and the sides of which

CREEDE

At a New Mining Camp

it has tramped into mud and covered with hundreds of little pine-boxes of houses and log-cabins, and the simple quadrangles of four planks which mark a building site. In front of you is a village of fresh pine. There is not a brick, a painted front, nor an awning in the whole town. It is like a city of fresh card-board, and the pine shanties seem to trust for support to the rocky sides of the gulch into which they have squeezed themselves. In the street are ox-teams, mules, men, and donkeys loaded with ore, crowding each other familiarly, and sinking knee-deep in the mud. Furniture and kegs of beer, bedding and canned provisions, clothing and half-open packing-cases, and piles of raw lumber are heaped up in front of the new stores— or those still to be built—stores of canvas only, stores with canvas tops and foundations of logs, and houses with the Leadville front, where the upper boards have been left square instead of following the sloping angle of the roof.

It is more like a circus-tent, which has sprung up overnight and which may be removed on the morrow, than a town, and you cannot but feel that the people about you are a part of the show. A great shaft of rock that rises hundreds of feet above the lower town gives the little village at its base an absurdly pushing, impudent air, and the silence of the mountains around from ten to fourteen thousand feet high, makes the confusion of hammers and the cries of the drivers swearing at their mules in the mud and even the random blasts from the mines futile and ridiculous. It is more strange and fantastic at night, when it appears to one looking down from half-way up the mountain like a camp of gypsies at the foot of a cañon. On the raw pine fronts shine electric lights in red and blue globes, mixing with the hot, smoky glare rising from the saloons and gambling-houses, and striking upward far enough to show the signs of The Holy Moses Saloon, The Theatre Comique, The Keno, and The Little Delmonico against the face of the great rock at their back doors, but only suggesting the greater mass of it which towers majestically above, hidden somewhere in the night. It is as incongruous as an excursion boat covered with colored lights, and banging out popular airs at the base of the Palisades.

The town of Creede is in what is known as the King

HOW LAND IS CLAIMED FOR BUILDING—PLANKS NAILED TOGETHER AND RESTING ON FOUR STUMPS

At a New Mining Camp

Solomon district; it is three hundred and twenty miles from Denver, and lies directly in the pathway of the Great Divide. Why it was not discovered sooner, why, indeed, there is one square foot of land in Colorado containing silver not yet discovered, is something which the Eastern mind cannot grasp. Colorado is a State, not a country, and in that State the mines of Leadville, Aspen, Ouray, Clear Creek County, Telluride, Boulder, Silverton, and Cripple Creek, have yielded up in the last year forty million dollars. If the State has done that much, it can do more; and I could not understand why any one in Colorado should remain contentedly at home selling ribbons when there must be other mines to be had for the finding. A prospector is, after all, very much like a tramp, but with a knowledge of minerals, a pick, rations, a purpose, and— hope. We know how many tramps we have in the East; imagine, then, all of these, instead of wandering lazily and purposelessly from farm-house to farm-house, stopping instead to hammer at a bit of rock, or stooping to pick up every loose piece they find. One would think that with a regular army like this searching everywhere in Colorado no one acre of it would by this time have remained unclaimed. But this new town of Creede, once known only as Willow Gap, was discovered but twenty months ago, and it was not until December last that the railway reached it, and, as I have said, there is not a station there yet.

N. C. Creede was a prospector who had made some money in the Monarch district before he came to Willow Gap; he began prospecting there on Campbell, now Moses Mount, with G. L. Smith, of Salida. One of the two picked up a piece of rock so full of quartz that they sunk a shaft immediately below the spot where they had found the stone. According to all known laws, they should have sunk the shaft at the spot from which the piece of rock had become detached, or from whence it had presumably rolled. It was as absurd to dig for silver where they did dig as it would be to sink a shaft in Larimer Street, in Denver, because one had found a silver quarter lying in the roadway. But they dug the shaft; and when they looked upon the result of the first day's work, Smith cried, "Great God!" and Creede said, "Holy Moses!" and the Holy Moses Mine was named. While I was in Creede that gentleman was offered one million two hundred and fifty thousand dollars for his share of this mine, and declined it. After that my interest in him fell away. Any man who will live in a log house at the foot of a mountain, and drink melted snow any longer than he has to do so, or refuse that much money for *anything,* when he could live in the Knickerbocker Flats, and drive forth in a private hansom with rubber tires, is no longer an object of public interest.

But his past history is the history of the town. Creede and his partner knew they had a mine, but had no money to work it. So they applied to David S. Moffatt, the president of the Rio Grande Railroad, which has a track to Wagon Wheel Gap only ten miles away, and Moffatt and others formed the Holy Moses Mining Company, and secured a bond on the property at seventy thousand dollars. As soon as this was known, the invasion of Willow Gap began. It was the story of Columbus and the egg. Prospectors, and provisions with which to feed them, came in on foot and on stages, and Creede began to grow. But no more mines were found at once, and the railroad into the town was slow in coming, and many departed, leaving their posts and piles of rock to mark their claims. But

THE "HOLY MOSES" MINE

At a New Mining Camp

last June Creede received a second boom, and in a manner which heaps ridicule and scorn upon the scientific knowledge of engineers and mining experts, and which shows that luck, chance, and the absurd vagaries of fate are factors of success upon which a prospector should depend.

Ralph Granger and Eri Buddenbock ran a butcher shop at Wagon Wheel Gap. "The" Renninger, of Patiro, a prospector with no tools or provisions, asked them to grubstake him, as it is called when a man of capital furnishes a man of adventure with bacon, flour, a pick, and three or four donkeys, and starts him off prospecting, with the understanding that he is to have one-tenth of what he finds. Renninger asked Jule Haas to join him, and they departed together. One day the three burros disappeared, and wandered off many miles, with Renninger in hot and profane pursuit until they reached Bachelor Mountain, where he overtook them. But they liked Bachelor Mountain, and Renninger, failing to dislodge them with either rocks or kicks, seated himself to await their pleasure, and began to chip casually at the nearest rock. He struck a vein showing mineral in such rich quantities that he asked Creede to come up and look at it. Creede looked at it, and begged Renninger to define his claim at once. Renninger, offering up thanks to the three donkeys, did so, and named it the "Last Chance." Then Creede located next to this property, shoulder to shoulder, and named his claim the "Amethyst." These names are merely names to you; they mean nothing; in Colorado you speak them in a whisper, and they sound like the Standard Oil Company or the Koh-i-noor diamond. Haas was bought off for ten thousand dollars. He went to Germany to patronize the people in the little German village from which he came with his great wealth; four months later Renninger, and Buddenbock, who had staked him, sold their thirds for seventy thousand dollars each; a few days later Granger was offered one hundred thousand dollars for his third, and said he thought he would hold on to it. When I was there, the Chance was putting out one hundred and eighty thousand dollars per month. This shows that Granger was wiser in his generation than Haas.

At the time I visited Creede it was quite impossible to secure a bed in any of the hotels or lodging-houses. The Pullman cars were the only available sleeping-places, and rented out their berths for the night they laid over at the mining camp. But even in these, sleeping was precarious, as one gentleman found the night after my arrival. He was mistaken for another man who had picked up a bag of gold-dust from a faro table at Little Delmonico's, and who had fled into the night. After shooting away the pine-board façade in the Mint gambling-house in which he was supposed to have sought shelter, several citizens followed him on to the sleeping-car, and, of course, pulled the wrong man out of his berth, and stood him up in the aisle in front of four revolvers, while the porter and the other wrong men shivered under their blankets, and begged them from behind the closed curtains to take him outside before they began shooting. The camp was divided in its opinion on the following morning as to whether the joke was on the passenger or on the hasty citizens.

A colony of younger sons from the East took pity upon me, and gave me a bunk in their Grub Stake cabin, where I had the satisfaction of watching the son of a president of the Somerset Club light the fire with kerosene while the rest of us remained under the blankets and asked him to

At a New Mining Camp

DEBATABLE GROUND—A WARNING TO TRESPASSERS

be careful. They were a most hospitable, cheerful lot. When it was so cold that the ice was frozen in the tin basin, they would elect to remain in bed all day, and would mark up the prices they intended to ask for their lots and claims one hundred dollars each; and then, considering this a fair day's wages for a hard day's work, would go warmly to sleep again. It is interesting, chiefly to mothers and sisters—for the fathers and brothers have an unsympathetic way of saying, "It is the best thing for him"—to discover how quickly such carefully bred youths as one constantly meets in the mining camps and ranches of the West can give up the comforts and habits of years and fit into their surroundings. It is instructive and hopeful to watch a young man who can and has ordered numerous dinners at Bignon's, composing a dessert of bread and molasses, or to see how neatly a Yale graduate of one year's standing can sweep the mud from the cabin floor without spreading it. If people at home could watch these young exiles gorge themselves with their letters, a page at a time, and then go over them again word by word, they would write early and often; and if the numerous young women of New York and Boston could know that their photographs were the only bright spots in a log-cabin filled with cartridge-belts, picks, saddles, foot-ball sweaters, patent-medicine bottles, and three-months-old magazines, they would be moved with great content.

One cannot always discern the true character of one's neighbors in the West. "Dress," as Bob Acres says, "does make a difference." There were four very rough-looking men of different ages sitting at a table near me in one of the restaurants or "eating-houses" of Creede. They had marked out a map on the soiled table-cloth with the point of an iron fork, and one of them was laying down the law concerning it. There seemed to be a dispute concerning the lines of the claim or the direction in which the vein ran. It was no business of mine, and there was so much of that talk that I should not have been attracted to them, except that I expected from their manner they might at any moment come to blows or begin shooting. I finished before they did, and as I passed the table over which they leaned scowling excitedly, the older man cried, with his finger on the map:

"Then Thompson passed the ball back to me—no, not your Thompson; Thompson of '79 I mean—and I carried it down the field all the way to the twenty-five-yard line.

A MINING CAMP COURT-HOUSE

At a New Mining Camp

Canfield, who was playing full, tackled me; but I shook him off, and—"

I should have liked to wait and hear whether or not he made his touch-down.

The shaft of the Last Chance Mine is at the top of the Bachelor Mountain, and one has to climb and slip for an hour and a half to reach it. A very nice Yale boy guided me there, and seemed as willing as myself to sit down in the snow every ten minutes and look at the scenery. But we saw much more of the scenery than of the mine, because there was more of it to see, and there was no general manager to prevent us from looking as long as we liked. The trail led over fallen logs and up slippery rocks caked with ice and through drifts of snow higher than one's head, and the pines accompanied us all the way with branches bent to the mountain-side with the weight of the snow, and a cold, cheery mountain stream appeared and disappeared from under long bridges of ice and mocked at us for our slow progress. But we gave it a very close race coming down. Sometimes we walked in the cold, dark shadows of the pines, where hardly a ray of sunlight came, and again the trail would cross a landslide, and the wind brought strong odors of the pine and keen, icy blasts from the snow-capped ranges which stretched before us for fifty miles, and we could see Creede lying at our feet like a box of spilled jackstraws. Every now and then we met long lines of burros carrying five bags of ore each, with but twenty dollars' worth of silver scattered through each load, and we could hear the voice of the driver from far up above and the tinkle of the bell as they descended upon us. Sometimes they made way for us or halted timidly with curious, patient eyes, and sometimes they shouldered us promptly backward into three feet of snow. It was a lonely, impressive journey, and the wonderful beauty and silence of the mountain made words impertinent. And, again, we would come upon a solitary prospector tapping at the great rock in front of him, and only stopping to dip his hot face and blistered hands into the snow about him, before he began to drive the steel bar again with the help which hope gave him. His work but for this ingredient would seem futile, foolish, and impossible. Why, he would ask himself, should I work against this stone safe day after day only to bore a hole in its side as minute as a nail's point in the front of a house, and a thousand rods, probably, from where the hole should be? And then hope tells him that perhaps the very next stroke will make him a millionaire like Creede, and so he makes the next stroke, and the next, and the next.

If ever I own a silver mine, I am going to have it situated at the base of a mountain, and not at the top. I would not care to take that journey we made to the Chance every day. I would rather sit in the office below and read reports. After one gets there, the best has been seen; for the general manager of the Last Chance Mine, to whom I had a letter of introduction, and indeed all the employés, guarded their treasure with the most praiseworthy and faithful vigilance. It was evident that they were quietly determined among themselves to resist any attempt on the part of the Yale man and myself to carry away the shaft with us. We could have done so only over their dead bodies. The general manager confounded me with the editor of the *Saturday Night*, which he said he reads, and which certainly ought to account for several things. I expected to be led into a tunnel, and to be shown delicate

At a New Mining Camp

veins of white silver running around the sides, which one could cut out with a penknife and make into scarf-pins and watch guards. If not, from whence, then, do the nuggets come that the young and disappointed lover sends as a wedding present to the woman who should have married him, when she marries some other man who has sensibly remained in the East—a present, indeed, which has always struck me as extremely economical, and much cheaper than standing-lamps. But I saw no silver nuggets. One of the workmen showed us a hole in the side of the mountain which he assured us was the Last Chance Mine, and that out of this hole one hundred and eighty thousand dollars came every month. He then handed us a piece of red stone and a piece of black stone, and said that when these two stones were found together silver was not far off. To one thirsting for a sight of the precious metal this was about as satisfying as being told that after the invitations had been sent out and the awning stretched over the sidewalk there was a chance of a dance in the neighborhood. I was also told that the veins lie between walls of porphyry and trachyte, but that there is not a distinctly marked difference, as the walls resemble each other closely. This may or may not be true; it is certainly not interesting, and I regret that I cannot satisfy the mining expert as to the formation of the mine, or tell him whether or not the vein is a heavy galena running so much per cent. of lead, or a dry silicious ore, or whether the ore bodies were north and south, and are or are not true fissures, and at what angle the contact or body veins cut these same fissures. All of this I should have ascertained had the general manager been more genial; but we cannot expect one man to combine the riches of Montezuma and the graces of Chesterfield. One is sure to destroy the other.

The social life of Creede is much more interesting than outputs and ore values. There were several social functions while I was there which tend to show the happy spirit of the place. There was a prize-fight at Billy Woods', a pie-eating match at Kernan's, a Mexican circus in the bottom near Wagon Wheel Gap, a religious service at Watrous and Bannigan's gambling-house, and the first wedding in the history of the town. I was sorry to miss this last, especially as three prominent citizens, misunderstanding the purpose of my visit to Creede, took the trouble to scour the mountain-side for me in order that I might photograph the wedding party in a group, which I should have been delighted to do. The bride was the sister of Billy Woods's barkeeper, and "Stony" Sargeant, a faro-dealer at "Soapy" Smith's, was the groom. The Justice of the Peace, whose name I forget, performed the ceremony, and Edward De Vinne, the Tramp Poet, offered a few appropriate and well-chosen remarks, after which Woods and Smith, who run rival gambling-houses, outdid each other in the extravagant practice of "opening wine." All of these are prominent citizens, and the event was memorable.

I met several of these prominent citizens while in Creede, and found them affable. Billy Woods fights, or used to fight, at two hundred and ten pounds, and rejoices in the fact that a New York paper once devoted five columns to his personality. His reputation saves him the expense of paying men to keep order. Bob Ford, who shot Jesse James, was another prominent citizen of my acquaintance. He does not look like a desperado, but has a loutish

VALUABLE REAL ESTATE

apologetic air, which is explained by the fact that he shot Jesse James in the back, when the latter was engaged in the innocent work of hanging a picture on the wall. Ford never quite recovered from the fright he received when he found out who it was that he had killed. "Bat" Masterden was of an entirely different class. He dealt for Watrous, and has killed twenty-eight men, once three together. One night when he was off duty I saw a drunken man slap his face, and the silence was so great that we could hear the electric light sputter in the next room; but Masterden only laughed, and told the man to come back and do it again when he was sober. "Troublesome Tom" Cady acted as a capper for "Soapy" Smith, and played the shell game during the day. He was very grateful to me for teaching him a much superior method in which the game is played in the effete East. His master, "Soapy" Smith, was a very bad man indeed, and hired at least twelve men to lead the prospector with a little money, or the tenderfoot who had just arrived, up to the numerous tables in his gambling-saloon, where they were robbed in various ways so openly that they deserved to lose all that was taken from them.

There were also some very good shots at Creede, and some very bad ones. Of these latter was Mr. James Powers, who emptied his revolver and Rab Brothers' store at the same time without doing any damage. He explained that he was crowded and wanted more room. The most delicate shooting was done by the Louisiana Kid—I don't know what his other name was—who was robbed in Soapy Smith's saloon, and was put out when he expostulated. He waited patiently until one of Smith's men named Farnham, appeared, and then, being more intent in showing his skill than on killing Farnham, shot the thumb off his right hand as it rested on the trigger. Farnham shifted his pistol to his left hand, with which he shot equally well, but before he could fire the Kid shot the thumb off that hand too.

This is, of course, Creede at night. It is not at all a dangerous place, and the lawlessness is scattered and mild. There was only one street, and as no one cared to sit on the edge of a bunk in a cold room at night, the gambling-houses were crowded in consequence every evening. It was simply because there was nowhere else to go. The majority of the citizens used them as clubs, and walked from one to the other talking claims and corner lots, and dived down into their pockets for specimens of ore which they passed around for examination. Others went there to keep warm, and still others to sleep in the corner until they were put out. The play was never high. There was so much of it, though, that it looked very bad and wicked and rough, but it was quite harmless. There were no sudden oaths, nor parting of the crowd, and pistol-shots or gleaming knives—or, at least, but seldom. The women who frequented these places at night, in spite of their sombreros and flannel shirts and belts, were a most unpicturesque and unattractive element. They were neither dashing and bold, nor remorseful and repentant.

They gambled foolishly, and laughed when they won, and told the dealer he cheated when they lost. The men occasionally gave glimpses of the life which Bret Harte made dramatic and picturesque—the women, never. The most uncharacteristic thing of the place, and one which was Bret Hartish in every detail, was the service held in Watrous and Bannigan's gambling-saloon. The hall is a

UPPER CREEDE

At a New Mining Camp

very long one with a saloon facing the street, and keno tables, and a dozen other games in the gambling-room beyond. When the doors between the two rooms are held back they make a very large hall. A clergyman asked Watrous if he could have the use of the gambling-hall on Sunday night. The house was making about three hundred dollars an hour, and Watrous calculated that half an hour would be as much as he could afford towards the collection. He mounted a chair and said, "Boys, this gentleman wants to make a few remarks to you of a religious nature. All the games at that end of the hall will stop, and you want to keep still."

The clergyman stood on the platform of the keno outfit, and the greater part of the men took the seats around it, toying with the marking cards scattered over the table in front of them, while the men in the saloon crowded the doorway from the swinging-doors to the bar, and looked on with curious and amused faces. At the back of the room the roulette wheel clicked and the ball rolled. The men in this part of the room who were playing lowered their voices, but above the voice of the preacher one could hear the clinking of the silver and the chips, and the voice of the boy at the wheel calling, "seventeen and black, and twenty-eight and black again and—keep the ball rolling, gentlemen — and four and red." There are two electric lights in the middle of the hall and a stove; the men were crowded closely around this stove, and the lamps shone through the smoke on their tanned upturned faces and on the white excited face of the preacher above them. There was the most excellent order, and the collection was very large. I asked Watrous how much he lost by the interruption.

"Nothing," he said, quickly, anxious to avoid the appearance of good; "I got it all back at the bar."

Of the inner life of Creede I saw nothing; I mean the real business of the place—the speculation in real estate and in mines. Capitalists came every day, and were carried off up the mountains to look at a hole in the ground, and down again to see the assay tests of the ore taken from it. Prospectors scoured the sides of the mountains from sundawn to sunset, and at night their fires lit up the range, and their little heaps of stone and their single stick, with their name scrawled on it in pencil, made the mountains look like great burying-grounds. All of the land within two miles of Creede was claimed by these simple proofs of ownership—simple, yet as effectual as a parchment sealed and signed. When the snow has left the mountains, and these claims can be worked, it will be time enough to write the real history of the rise or fall of Creede.

IV

A THREE-YEAR-OLD CITY

IV

A THREE-YEAR-OLD CITY

THE only interest which the East can take in Oklahoma City for some time to come must be the same as that with which one regards a portrait finished by a lightning crayon artist, "with frame complete," in ten minutes. We may have seen better portraits and more perfect coloring, but we have never watched one completed, as it were, "while you wait." People long ago crowded to see Master Betty act, not because there were no better actors in those days, but because he was so very young to do it so very well. It was as a freak of nature, a Josef Hoffman of the drama, that they considered him, and Oklahoma City must content itself with being only of interest as yet as a freak of our civilization.

After it has decided which of the half-dozen claimants to each of its town sites is the only one, and the others have stopped appealing to higher and higher courts, and have left the law alone and have reduced their attention strictly to business, and the city has been burned down once or twice, and had its Treasurer default and its Mayor impeached, and has been admitted to the National Baseball League, it may hope to be regarded as a full-grown rival city; but at present, as far as it concerns the far East, it

The West from a Car-Window

OKLAHOMA CITY ON THE DAY OF THE OPENING

is interesting chiefly as a city that grew up overnight, and did in three years or less what other towns have accomplished only after half a century. The history of its pioneers and their invasion of their undiscovered country not only shows how far the West is from the East, but how much we have changed our ways of doing things from the days of the Pilgrim Fathers to those of the modern pilgrims, the "boomers" and "sooners" of the end of the century. We have seen pictures in our school-books, and pictures which Mr. Boughton has made for us, of the *Mayflower's* people kneeling on the shore, the long, anxious voyage behind them, and the "rock-bound coast" of their new home before them, with the Indians looking on doubtfully from behind the pine-trees. It makes a very interesting picture—those stern-faced pilgrims in their knickerbockers and broad white collars; each man strong in the consciousness that he has resisted persecution

A Three-Year-Old City

and overcome the perils of the sea, and is ready to meet the perils of an unknown land. I should like you to place in contrast with this the opening of Oklahoma Territory to the new white settlers three years ago. These modern pilgrims stand in rows twenty deep, separated from the promised land not by an ocean, but by a line scratched in the earth with the point of a soldier's bayonet. The long row toeing this line are bending forward, panting with excitement, and looking with greedy eyes towards the new Canaan, the women with their dresses tucked up to their knees, the men stripped of coats and waistcoats for the coming race. And then, a trumpet call, answered by a thousand hungry yells from all along the line, and hundreds of men and women on foot and on horseback break away across the prairie, the stronger pushing down the weak, and those on horseback riding over and in some cases killing those on foot, in a mad, unseemly race for something which they are getting for nothing. These pilgrims do not drop on one knee to give thanks decorously, as did Columbus according to the twenty-dollar bills, but fall on both knees, and hammer stakes into the ground and pull them up again, and drive them down somewhere else, at a place which they hope will eventually become a corner lot facing the post-office, and drag up the next man's stake, and threaten him with a Winchester because he is on *their* land, which they have owned for the last three minutes. And there are no Indians in this scene. They have been paid one dollar and twenty-five cents an acre for the land, which is worth five dollars an acre as it lies, before a spade has been driven into it or a bit of timber cut, and they are safely out of the way.

Oklahoma Territory, which lies in the most fertile part

of the Indian Territory, equally distant from Kansas and Texas, was thrown open to white settlers at noon on the 22d of April, 1889. To appreciate the Oklahoma City of this day, it is necessary to go back to the Oklahoma of three years ago. The city at that time consisted of a railroad station, a section house and water-tank, the home of the railroad agent, and four other small buildings. The rest was prairie-land, with low curving hills covered with high grass and bunches of thick timber; this as far as the eye could see, and nothing else. This land, which is rich and black and soft, and looks like chocolate where the plough has turned the sod, was thrown open by the proclamation of the President to white settlers, who could on such a day, at such an hour, " enter and occupy it" for homestead holdings. A homestead holding is one hundred and sixty acres of land. The proclamation said nothing about town sites, or of the division of town sites into "lots" for stores, or of streets and cross-streets. But several bodies of men in different parts of Kansas prepared plans long before the opening, for a town to be laid out around the station, the water-tank, and the other buildings where Oklahoma City now stands, and had their surveyors and their blue prints hidden away in readiness for the 22d of April. All of those who intended to enter this open-to-all-comers race for land knew that the prairie around the station would be laid out into lots. Hence that station and other stations which in time would become cities were the goals for which over forty thousand people raced from the borders of the new Territory. So many of these "beat the pistol" on the start and reached the goal first that, in consequence, the efforts ever since to run this race over again through the law courts has kept Oklahoma City from growing

FIVE DAYS AFTER THE OPENING

A Three-Year-Old City

with even more marvellous rapidity than it already has done.

The Sunday before the 22d was a warm bright day, and promised well for the morrow. Soldiers and deputy marshals were the only living beings in sight around the station, and those who tried to descend from passing trains were pushed back again at the point of the bayonet. The course was being kept clear for the coming race. But freight cars loaded with raw lumber and furniture and all manner of household goods, as well as houses themselves, ready to be put together like the joints of a trout rod, were allowed free entry, and stood for a mile along the side-track awaiting their owners, who were hugging the border lines from fifteen to thirty miles away. Captain D. F. Stiles, of the Tenth Infantry, who had been made provost marshal of the new Territory, and whose soldiers guarded the land before and maintained peace after the invasion, raised his telescope at two minutes to twelve on the eventful 22d of April, and saw nothing from the station to the horizon but an empty green prairie of high waving grass. It would take the first horse (so he and General Merritt and his staff in their private car on the side-track decided) at least one hour and a quarter to cover the fifteen miles from the nearest border. They accordingly expected to catch the first glimpse of the leaders in the race with their glasses in about half an hour. The signal on the border was a trumpet call given by a cavalryman on a white horse, which he rode in a circle in order that those who were too far away to hear the trumpet might see that it had been sounded. A like signal was given at the station; but before it had died away, and *not* half an hour later, five hundred men sprang from the long grass, dropped from the branches of trees, crawled from under freight cars and out of cañons and ditches, and the blank prairie became alive with men running and racing about like a pack of beagles that have suddenly lost a hot trail.

Fifteen minutes after twelve the men of the Seminole Land and Town Company were dragging steel chains up the street on a run, the red and white barber poles and the transits were in place all over the prairie, and neat little rows of stakes stretched out in regular lines to mark where they hoped the town might be. At twenty minutes after twelve over forty tents were in position, and the land around them marked out by wooden pegs. This was the work of the "sooners," as those men were called who came into the Territory too soon, not for their own interests, but for the interests of other people. At a quarter past one the Rev. James Murray and a Mr. Kincaid, who represented the Oklahoma Colony, stopped a sweating horse and creaking buggy and hammered in their first stakes. They had left the border line exactly at noon, and had made the fifteen miles at the rate of five minutes per mile. Four minutes later J. H. McCortney and Colonel Harrison, of Kansas, arrived from the Canadian River, having whipped their horses for fifteen miles, and the mud from the river was over the hubs of the wheels. The first train from the south reached the station at five minutes past two, and unloaded twenty-five hundred people. They scattered like a stampeded herd over the prairie, driving in their little stakes, and changing their minds about it and driving them in again at some other point. There were already, even at this early period of the city's history, over three different men on each lot of ground, each sitting by the stake bearing his name, and each calling the other a "sooner," and therefore one ineli-

FOUR WEEKS AFTER THE OPENING

A Three-Year-Old City

gible to hold land, and many other names of more ancient usage.

But there was no blood shed even during the greatest excitement of that feverish afternoon. This was in great part due to the fact that the provost marshal confiscated all the arms he saw. At three o'clock the train from the north arrived with hundreds more hanging from the steps and crowding the aisles. The sight of so many others who had beaten them in the race seemed to drive these latecomers almost frantic, and they fell over one another in their haste, and their race for the choicest lots was like a run on a bank when no one knows exactly where the bank is. One young woman was in such haste to alight that she crawled out of the car window, and as soon as she reached the solid earth beneath, drove in her stake and claimed all the land around it. This was part of the military reservation, and the soldiers explained this to her, or tried to, but she was suspicious of every one, and remained seated by her wooden peg until nightfall. She could just as profitably have driven it into the centre of Union Square. Another woman stuck up a sign bearing the words, "A Soldier's Widow's Land," and was quite confident that the chivalry of the crowd would respect that title. Captain Stiles told her that he thought it would not, and showed her a lot of ground still unclaimed that she could have, but she refused to move. The lot he showed her is now on the main street, in the centre of the town, and the lot she was finally forced to take is three miles out of the city in the prairie. Another woman drove her stake between the railroad ties, and said it would take a locomotive and a train of cars to move *her*. One man put his stake in the very centre of the lot sites laid out by the surveyors, and claimed the one hundred and sixty acres around for his homestead holding. They explained to him that he could only have as much land as would make a lot in the town site, and that if he wanted one hundred and sixty acres, must locate it outside of the city limits. He replied that the proclamation said nothing about town sites.

"But, of course," he went on, "if you people want to build a city around my farm, I have no objections. I don't care for city life myself, and I am going to turn this into a vegetable garden. Maybe, though, if you want it very bad, I *might* sell it."

He and the city fought it out for months, and, for all I know, are at it still. At three o'clock, just three hours after the Territory was invaded, the Oklahoma Colony declared the polls open, and voting began for Mayor and City Clerk. About four hundred people voted. Other land companies at once held public meetings and protested against this election. Each land company was mapping out and surveying the city to suit its own interests, and every man and woman was more or less of a land company to himself or herself, and the lines and boundaries and streets were intersecting and crossing like the lines of a dress pattern. Night came on and put a temporary hush to this bedlam, and six thousand people went to sleep in the open air, the greater part of them without shelter. There was but one well in the city, and word was brought to Captain Stiles about noon of the next day that the water from this was being sold by a speculative gentleman at five cents per pint, and that those who had no money were suffering. Captain Stiles found the well guarded by a faro-dealer with a revolver. He had a tin basin between his knees filled with nickels. He argued that he owned the lot on which the

CAPTAIN D. F. STILES

water stood, and had as much private right to the well as to a shaft that led down to a silver or an iron mine. Captain Stiles threw him and his basin out at some distance on to the prairie, and detailed a corporal's guard to see that every one should get as much water as he wanted.

During the morning there was an attempt made to induce the surveyors of the different land companies to combine and readjust their different plans, but without success. Finally, at three o'clock, the people came together in desperation to decide what was to be done, and, after an amusing and exciting mass-meeting, fourteen unhappy and prominent citizens were selected to agree upon an entirely new site. The choosing of this luckless fourteen was accomplished by general nomination, each nominee having first to stand upon a box that he might be seen and considered by the crowd. They had to submit to such embarrassing queries as, "Where are you from, and why did you have to leave?" "Where did you get that hat?" "What is your excuse for living?" "Do you live with your folks, or does your wife support you?" "What was your other name before you came here?" The work of this committee began on the morrow, and as they slowly proceeded along the new boundary lines which they had mapped out, they were followed by all of those of the population, which now amounted to ten thousand souls, who thought it safe to leave their claims. As a rule, they found three men on each lot, and it was their pleasant duty to decide to which of these the lot belonged. They did this on the evidence of those who had lots near by. In many cases, each member of each family had selected a lot for himself, and this complicated matters still farther. The crowd at last became so importunate and noisy that the committee asked for a military guard, which was given them, and the crowd after that was at least kept off the lot they were considering. The committee met with no real opposition until it reached Main Street on Saturday, the fifth day of the city's life, where those who had settled along the lines laid down by the Seminole Land Company pulled up the stakes of the citizens' committee as soon as they were driven down. For a time it looked very much as though the record of peace was about to be broken along with other things, but a committee of five men from each side of the street decided the matter at a meeting held

A Three-Year-Old City

that afternoon. At this same public meeting articles of confederation were adopted, and a temporary Mayor, Recorder, Police Judge, and other city officials were appointed, who were to receive one dollar for their services. This meeting closed with cheers and with the singing of the doxology.

The next day was Sunday, and was more or less observed. Captain Stiles visited the gamblers, who swarmed about the place in great numbers, and asked them to close their tables, which they did, although he had no power to stop them if they had not wished to do so. In the afternoon two separate religious services were held, to which the people were called by a trumpeter from the infantry camp.

This is, in brief, the history of the first week of this new city. There were, considering the circumstances, but few disturbances, and there was no drunkenness. This is disappointing, but true. Both came later. But at the first no one cared to shoot the gentleman on the other end of his lot, lest the man on the next lot might prove to be a relative of his, and begin to shoot too. Later on, when everybody became better acquainted, the shooting was more general. They could not easily get anything to drink, as Captain Stiles seized all the liquor, and when it came in vessels of unmanageable size that could not be stored away, spilled it over the prairie. In two weeks over one thousand buildings were enclosed, and there would have been more if there had been more lumber.

It would be interesting to follow the course of this skyrocket among cities up to the present day, and tell how laws were evolved and courts established, and the complexities of the situation disentangled; but that is work for one of the many bright young men who write monographs on economic subjects at the Johns Hopkins University. It is just the sort of work in which they delight, and which they do well, and they will find many "oldest inhabitants" of this three-year-old city to take equal delight in telling them of these early days, and in explaining the rights and wrongs of their individual lawsuits against their city and their neighbors.

It is impossible, in considering the founding of Oklahoma, to overrate the services of Captain Stiles. Seldom has the case of the right man in the right place been so happily demonstrated. He was particularly fitted to the work, although I doubt if the Government knew of it before he was sent there, so apt is it to get the square peg in the round hole, unless the square peg's uncle is a Senator. But Cap-

POST-OFFICE, APRIL 22, 1889

A Three-Year-Old City

tain Stiles, when he was a lieutenant, had ruled at Waco, Texas, during the reconstruction period, and the questions and difficulties that arose after the war in that raw community fitted him to deal with similar ones in the construction of Oklahoma. He was and is intensely unpopular with the worst element in Oklahoma, and the better element call him blessed, and have presented him with a three-hundred dollar gold cane, which is much too fine for him to carry except in clear weather. This is the way public sentiment should be adjusted. Personal bravery had, I think, as much to do with his success as the readiness with which he met the difficulties he had to solve at a moment's consideration. Several times he walked up to the muzzles of revolvers with which desperadoes covered him and wrenched them out of their owners' hands. He never interfered between the people and the civil law, and resisted the temptation of misusing his authority in a situation where a weaker man would have lost his head and abused his power. He was constantly appealed to to settle disputes, and his invariable answer was, "I am not here to decide which of you owns that lot, but to keep peace between you until it is decided." In September of 1889 a number of disaffected citizens announced an election which was to overthrow those then in power, and Captain Stiles was instructed by his superior officers to prevent its taking place. This he did with a small force of men in the face of threats from the most dangerous element in the community of dynamite bombs and of a body of men armed with Winchesters who were to shoot him first and his men later. But in spite of this he visited and broke all the voting booths, wrested a Winchester from the hands of the man who pointed it at his heart through one of the windows of the polling-place, and finally charged the mob of five hundred men with twenty-five soldiers and his fighting surgeon, young Dr. Ives, and dispersed them uttterly. I heard these stories of him on every side, and I was rejoiced to think how well off our army must be in majors, that the people at Washington can allow one who has served through the war and on the border and in this unsettled Territory, and whose hair has grown white in the service, to still wear two bars on his shoulder-strap.

It is much more pleasant to write of these early days of Oklahoma City than of the Oklahoma City of the present, although one of its citizens would not find it so, for he regards his adopted home with a fierce local pride and jealousy almost equal to a Chicagoan's love for Chicago, which is saying a very great deal. But to the transient visitor Oklahoma City of to-day, after he has recovered from the shock its extent and solidity give him, is dispiriting and unprofitable to a degree. This may partly be accounted for by the circumstance that his only means of entering it from the south by train is, or was at the time I visited it, at four o'clock in the morning. No one, after having been dragged out of his berth and dropped into a cold misty well of darkness, punctured only by the light from the brakeman's lantern and a smoking omnibus lamp, is in a mood to grow enthusiastic over the city about him. And the fact that the hotel is crowded, and that he must sleep with the barkeeper, does not tend to raise his spirits. I can heartily recommend this method of discouraging immigration to the authorities of any already overcrowded city.

But as the sun comes up, one sees the remarkable growth of this city—remarkable not only for its extent in so short

A Three-Year-Old City

POST-OFFICE, JULY 4, 1890

a period, but for the come-to-stay air about many of its buildings. There are stone banks and stores, and an opera-house, and rows of brick buildings with dwelling-rooms above, and in the part of the city where the people go to sleep hundreds of wooden houses, fashioned after the architecture of the sea-shore cottages of the Jersey coast; for the climate is mild the best part of the year. There are also churches of stone and brick and stained glass, and a flour-mill, and three or four newspapers, and courts of law, and boards of trade. But with all of these things, which show a steadily improving growth after the mushroom nature of its birth, Oklahoma City cannot or has not yet shaken off the attributes with which it was born, and which in a community founded by law and purchase would not exist. For speculation in land, whether in lots on the main street or in homestead holdings on the prairie, and the excitement of real estate transfers, and the battle for rights in the courts, seem to be the prevailing and ruling passion of the place. Gambling in real estate is as much in the air as is the spirit of the Louisiana State Lottery in New Orleans. Every one in Oklahoma City seems to live, in part at least, by transferring real estate to some one else, and the lawyers and real-estate agents live by helping them to do it. It reminded me of that happy island in the Pacific seas where every one took in every one else's washing. This may sound unfair, but it is not in the least exaggerated. The town swarms with lawyers, and is overrun with real-estate offices. The men you meet and the men you pass in the street are not discussing the weather or the crops or the news of the outside world, but you hear them say: "I'll appeal it, by God!" "I'll spend every cent I've got, sir!" "They're a lot of 'sooners,' and I can prove it!" or, "Ted Hillman's lot on Prairie Avenue, that he sold for two hundred dollars, rose to three hundred in one week, and Abner Brown says he won't take six hundred for it now."

This is only the natural and fitting outcome of the bungling, incomplete bill which, rushed through at the hot, hurried end of a session, authorized the opening of this territory. The President might with equal judgment have proclaimed that "The silver vaults of the United States Treasury will be opened on the 22d of April, when citizens can enter in and take away one hundred and sixty silver dollars each," without providing laws to prevent or punish those who entered before that date, or those who snatched more than their share. One would think that some distinction might have been made, in opening this new land, between those who came with family and money and stock, meaning to settle permanently, and those who took the morning train from Kansas in order to rush in and snatch a holding, only to sell it again in three hours and to return to their homes that night; between those who brought capital, and desperadoes and "boot-leggers" who came to make capital out of others. If the land was worth giving away, it was worth giving to those who would make the best use of it, and worth surrounding with at least as much order as that which distinguishes the fight of the Harvard Seniors for the flowers on Class day. They are going to open still more territory this spring, and in all probability the same confusion will arise and continue, and it is also probable that many persons in the East may be attracted by the announcements and advertisements of the "boomers" to this new land.

The West is always full of hope to the old man as well as to the young one, and the temptation to "own your own home" and to gain land for the asking is very great. But the Eastern man should consider the question very carefully. There is facing the passenger who arrives on the New York train at Sedalia a large black and white sign on which some philanthropist has painted "Go East, Young Man, Go East." One might write pages and not tell more than that sign does, when one considers where it is placed and for what purpose it is placed there.

A man in Oklahoma City when the day's work is done has before him a prospect of broad red clayey streets, muddy after rain, bristling with dust after a drought, with the sun setting at one end of them into the prairie. He can go to his cottage, or to "The Turf," where he can lose some money at faro, or he can sit in one of the hotels, which are the clubs of the city, and talk cattle to strangers and real estate to citizens, or he can join a lodge and talk real estate there. Once or twice a week a "show" makes a one-night stand at the opera-house. The schools are not good for his children as yet, and the society that he is willing his wife should enjoy is limited. On Sunday he goes to church, and eats a large dinner in the middle of the day, and walks up to the top of the hill to look over the prairie where he and many others would like to build, but which must remain empty until the twelve different disputants for each holding have stopped appealing to higher courts. This is actually the case, and the reason the city has not spread as others around it have done. As the Romans shortened their swords to extend their boundaries, so the people of Oklahoma City might cut down some of their higher courts and increase theirs.

I have given this sketch of Oklahoma City as it impressed itself on me, because I think any man who can afford a hall bedroom and a gas-stove in New York City is better off than he would be as the owner of one hundred and sixty acres on the prairie, or in one of these small so-called cities.

And the men who are at the head of affairs, who rose out of the six thousand in a week, and who have kept at the head ever since, if they had exerted the same energy, and showed the same executive ability and the same cleverness in a real city, would be real mayors, real merchants, and real "prominent citizens." They are now as men playing with children's toys or building houses of cards. Every

OKLAHOMA CITY TO-DAY—MAIN BROADWAY

now and then a Roger Q. Mills or a Henry W. Grady comes out of the South and West, and among these politicians and first citizens of Oklahóma City are men who only need a broader canvas and a greater opportunity to show what they can do. There are as many of these as there are uncouth "Sockless" Simpsons, or noisy Ingallses, and it is pathetic and exasperating to see men who would excel in a great metropolis, and who could live where they could educate their children *and* themselves, and be in touch with the world moving about them, even though they were not of it, wasting their energies in a desert of wooden houses in the middle of an ocean of prairie, where their point of view is bounded by the railroad tank and a barbwire fence. It depends altogether on the man. There are men who are just big enough to be leading citizens of a town of six thousand inhabitants, who are meant for nothing else, and it is just as well they should be satisfied with the unsettled existence around them; but it would be better for these others to be small men in a big city than big men on a prairie, where the organ in the front room is their art gallery, book-store, theatre, church, and school, and where the rustling grass of the prairie greets them in the morning and goes to bed with them at night.

V

RANCH LIFE IN TEXAS

V.

RANCH LIFE IN TEXAS

THE inhabited part of a ranch, the part of it on which the people who own it live, bears about the same proportion to the rest of the ranch as a light-house does to the ocean around it. And to an Eastern man it appears almost as lonely. Some light-houses are isolated in the ocean, some stand in bays, and some in harbors; and in the same proportion the ranches in Texas differ in size, from principalities to farms no larger than those around Jersey City. The simile is not altogether exact, as there are small bodies of men constantly leaving the "ranch-house" and wandering about over the range, sleeping wherever night catches them, and in this way different parts of the ranch are inhabited as well as the house itself. It is as if the light-house-keeper sent out a great number of row-boats to look after the floating buoys or to catch fish, and the men in those boats anchored whenever it grew dark, and returned to the light-house variously as best suited their convenience or their previous orders.

But it is the loneliness of the life that will most certainly first impress the visitor from closely built blocks of houses. Those who live on the ranches will tell you that they do not find it lonely, and that they grow so fond of the great breezy pastures about them that they become independent of the rest of mankind, and that a trip to the city once a year to go to the play and to "shop" is all they ask from the big world lying outside of the barb-wire fences. I am speaking now of those ranch-owners only who live on the range, and not of those who hire a foreman, and spend their time and money in the San Antonio Club. They are no more ranchmen than the absentee landlord who lives in his London house is a gentleman farmer.

The largest ranch in the United States, and probably in the world, owned by one person, is in Texas, and belongs to Mrs. Richard King, the widow of Captain Richard King. It lies forty-five miles south of Corpus Christi.

The ladies who come to call on Mrs. King drive from her front gate, over as good a road as any in Central Park, for ten miles before they arrive at her front door, and the butcher and baker and iceman, if such existed, would have to drive thirty miles from the back gate before they reached her kitchen. This ranch is bounded by the Corpus Christi Bay for forty miles, and by barb-wire for three hundred miles more. It covers seven hundred thousand acres in extent, and one hundred thousand head of cattle and three thousand broodmares wander over its different pastures.

This property is under the ruling of Robert J. Kleberg, Mrs. King's son-in-law, and he has under him a superintendent, or, as the Mexicans call one who holds that office, a major-domo, which is an unusual position for a major-domo, as this major-domo has the charge of three hundred cowboys and twelve hundred ponies reserved for their use. The "Widow's" ranch, as the Texans call it, is as carefully organized and moves on as conservative business principles as a bank. The cowboys do not ride over its range

THE RANCH-HOUSE ON THE KING RANCH, THE LARGEST RANGE OWNED BY ONE INDIVIDUAL IN THE UNITED STATES

with both legs at right angles to the saddle and shooting joyfully into the air with both guns at once. Neither do they offer the casual visitor a bucking pony to ride, and then roll around on the prairie with glee when he is shot up into the air and comes down on his collar-bone; they are more likely to bring him as fine a Kentucky thoroughbred as ever wore a blue ribbon around the Madison Square Garden. Neither do they shoot at his feet to see if he can dance. In this way the Eastern man is constantly finding his dearest illusions abruptly dispelled. It is also trying when the cowboys stand up and take off their sombreros when one is leaving their camp. There are cowboys and cowboys, and I am speaking now of those that I saw on the King ranch.

The thing that the wise man from the East cannot at first understand is how the one hundred thousand head of cattle wandering at large over the range are ever collected together. He sees a dozen or more steers here, a bunch of horses there, and a single steer or two a mile off, and even as he looks at them they disappear in the brush, and as far as his chance of finding them again would be, they might as well stand forty miles away at the other end of the ranch. But this is a very simple problem to the ranchman.

Mr. Kleberg, for instance, receives an order from a firm in Chicago calling for one thousand head of cattle. The breed of cattle which the firm wants is grazing in a corner of the range fenced in by barb-wire, and marked pale blue for convenience on a beautiful map blocked out in colors, like a patch-work quilt, which hangs in Mr. Kleberg's office. When the order is received, he sends a Mexican on a pony to tell the men near that particular pale blue pasture to round up one thousand head of cattle, and at the same time directs his superintendent to send in a few days as many cowboys to that pasture as are needed to "hold" one thousand head of cattle on the way to the railroad station. The boys on the pasture, which we will suppose is ten miles square, will take ten of their number and five extra ponies apiece, which one man leads, and from one to another of which they shift their saddles as men do in polo, and go directly to the water-tanks in the ten square miles of land. A cow will not often wander more than two and a half miles from water, and so, with the water-tank (which on the King ranch may be either a well with a wind-mill or a dammed cañon full of rain-water) as a rendezvous, the finding of the cattle is comparatively easy, and ten men can round up one thousand head in a day or two. When they have them all together, the cowboys who are to drive them to the station arrive, and take them off.

At the station the agent of the Chicago firm and the agent of the King ranch ride through the herd together, and if they disagree as to the fitness of any one or more of the cattle, an outsider is called in, and his decision is final. The cattle are then driven on to the cars, and Mr. Kleberg's responsibility is at an end.

In the spring there is a general rounding up, and thousands and thousands of steers are brought in from the different pastures, and those for which contracts have been made during the winter are shipped off to the markets, and the calves are branded.

Texas is the great breeding State from which the cattle are sent north to the better pasture land of Kansas, Montana, and Wyoming Territory, to be fattened up for the markets. The breeding goes on throughout the year, five

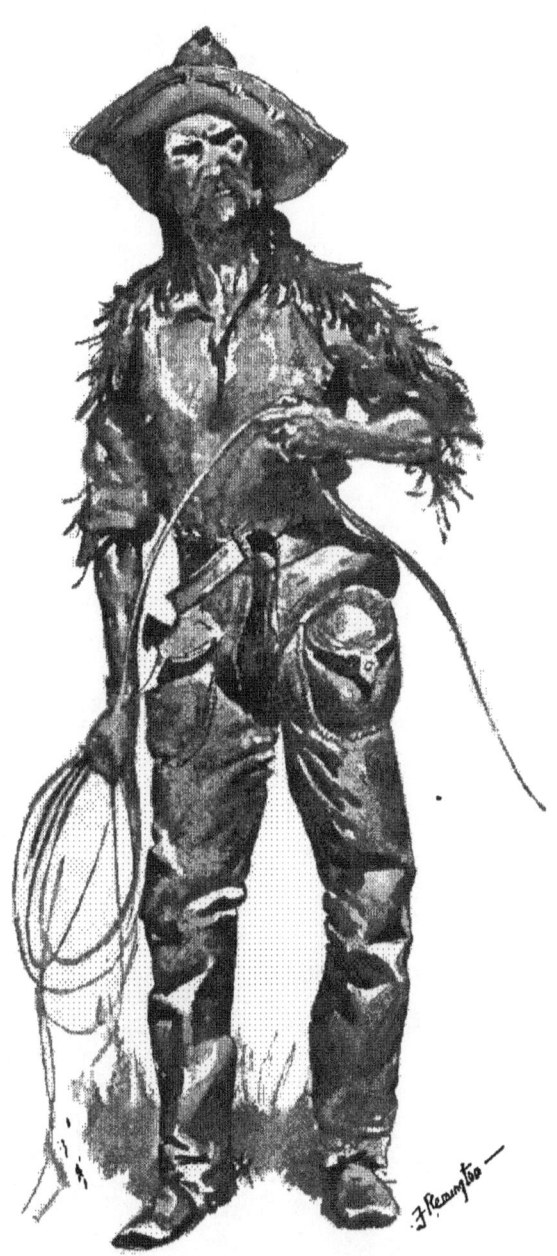

A SHATTERED IDOL

bulls being pastured with every three hundred cows, in pastures of from one thousand to ten thousand acres in extent. About ninety per cent. of the cows calve, and the branding of these calves is one of the most important duties of the spring work. They are driven into a pen through a wooden chute, and as they leave the chute are caught by the legs and thrown over on the side, and one of a dozen hot irons burning in an open fire is pressed against the flank, and, on the King ranch, on the nose.

An animal bearing one of the rough hall-marks of the ranchman is more respected than a dog with a silver collar around his neck, and the number of brands now registered in the State capital runs up to the thousands. On some ranches each of the family has his or her especial brand; and one young girl who came out in New York last winter is known throughout lower Texas only as "the owner of the Triangle brand," and is much respected in consequence, as it is borne by thousands of wandering cattle. The separating of the cattle at the spring round-up is accomplished on the King ranch by means of a cutting pen, a somewhat ingenious trap at the end of a chute. One end of this chute opens on the prairie, and the other runs into four different pens guarded by a swinging gate, so hung that by a movement of the foot by the man sitting over the gate the chute can be extended into any one of the four pens. With this mules, steers, horses, and ponies can be fed into the chute together, and each arrive in his proper pen until the number for which the different orders call is filled.

It is rather difficult to imagine one solitary family occupying a territory larger than some of the Eastern States —an area of territory that would in the East support a State capital, with a Governor and Legislature, and numer-

The West from a Car-Window

ous small towns, with competing railroad systems and rival baseball nines. And all that may be said of this side of the question of ranch life is that when we are within Mrs. King's house we would imagine it was one of twenty others touching shoulder to shoulder on Madison Avenue, and that the distant cry of the coyotes at night is all that tells us that the hansoms are not rushing up and down before the door.

SNAPPING A ROPE ON A HORSE'S FOOT

Ranch Life in Texas

In the summer this ranch is covered with green, and little yellow and pink flowers carpet the range for miles. It is at its best then, and is as varied and beautiful in its changes as the ocean.

The ranches that stretch along and away from the Rio Grande River are very different from this; they are owned by Mexicans, and every one on the ranch is a Mexican; the country is desolate here, and dead and dying cattle are everywhere.

No ranch-owner, whether he has fifty thousand or five hundred head of cattle, will ever attempt to help one that may be ailing or dying. This seems to one who has been taught the value of "three acres and a cow" the height of extravagance, and to show lack of feeling. But they will all tell you it is useless to try to save a starving or a sick animal, and also that it is not worth the trouble, there are so many more. In one place I saw where a horse had fallen on the trail, and the first man who passed had driven around it, and the next, and the next, until a new trail was made, and at the time I passed over this new trail, I could see the old one showing through the ribs of the horse's skeleton. In the East, I think, they would have at least pulled the horse out of the road.

But a live horse or steer is just as valuable in Texas as in the East—even more so.

The conductor on the road from Corpus Christi sprang from his chair in the baggage car one day, and shouted to the engineer that he must be careful, for we were on Major Fenton's range, and must look out for the major's prize bull; and the train continued at half speed accordingly until the conductor espied the distinguished animal well to the left, and shouted: "All right, Bill! We've passed him, let her out."

The West from a Car-Window

The Randado ranch is typical of the largest of the Mexican ranches which lie within the five hundred miles along the Rio Grande. It embraces eighty thousand acres, with twenty-five thousand head of cattle, and it has its store, its little mission, its tank, twenty or more adobe houses with thatched roofs, and its little graveyard. There is a post-office here, and a school, where very pretty little Mexicans recited proudly in English words of four letters. Around them lie the cactus and dense chaparral cut up with dusky trails, and the mail comes but twice a week. But every Saturday the vaqueros come in from the range, and there is dancing on the bare clay floor of one of the huts, and the school-master postmaster sings to them every evening on his guitar, and once a month the priest comes on horseback to celebrate mass in the adobe mission.

Around San Antonio are many ranches. These are more like large farms, and there are high trees and hills and a wonderful variety of flowers. There are also antelope and wild fowl for those who love to hunt, and the scalp of a coyote brings fifty cents to those who care for money; for the coyotes pull down the young calves. The life on the range is not at all lonely here, for the women on the ranch do not mind riding in twelve miles to a dance in San Antonio, and there are always people coming out from town to remain a day or two. The more successful of these ranches are like English country-houses in their free hospitality and in the constant changing of the guests.

Many of these about San Antonio are owned, in fact, by Englishmen, although a record of the failures of the English colonists of good family and of well-known youths from New York would make a book, and a very sad one. There was a whole colony of English families and unat-

tached younger sons at Boerne, just outside of San Antonio, a few years ago; but they preferred cutting to leg to cutting out cattle, and used the ponies to chase polo balls, and their money soon went, and they followed. Some went to England as prodigal sons, some to driving hacks and dealing faro, and others into the army. A few succeeded, and are still at Boerne, notably a cousin of Thomas Hughes, who founded the ill-fated English colony of Rugby, in Tennessee.

Of the New York men who came on to San Antonio, the two Jacob boys are more frequently and more heartily spoken of by the Texans than almost any other Eastern men who have been there. They did not, as the others so often do, hire a foreman, and spend their days in the San Antonio Club, but rode the ranch themselves, and could cut out and brand and rope with any of those born on a range. Their ranch, the Santa Marta, still flourishes, although they have become absentee landlords, and have given up chasing wild steers in Texas in favor of the foxes at Rockaway.

A ranch which marks the exception in the rule of failures of our English cousins is that of Alfred Giles in Kendal and Kerr counties. It covers about thirteen thousand acres, and a very fine breed of polled Angus cattle are bred on it. Indeed, the tendency all over Texas at present is to cultivate certain well-known breeds, and not, as formerly, to be content with the famous long-horned steer and the Texan pony. Mr. Giles's ranch, the Hillingdon, looks in the summer, when the imported Scotch cattle are grazing over it, like a bit out of the Lake country. Walnut, cherry, ash, and oak grow on this ranch, and the maidenhair-fern is everywhere, and the flowers are boundless in profusion and variety.

The coming of the barb-wire fence and the railroad killed

the cowboy as a picturesque element of recklessness and lawlessness in south-west Texas. It suppressed him and localized him and limited him to his own range, and made his revolver merely an ornament. Before the barb-wire fence appeared, the cattle wandered from one range to another, and the man of fifteen thousand acres would overstock, knowing that when his cattle could not find enough pasturage on his range they would move over to the range of his more prosperous neighbor. Consequently, when the men who could afford it began to fence their ranges, the smaller owners who had over-bred, saw that their cattle would starve, and so cut'the fences in order to get back to the pastures which they had used so long. This, and the shutting off of water-tanks and of long-used trails brought on the barb-wire fence wars which raged long and fiercely between the cowboys and fence men of rival ranches and the Texas Rangers. The barb-wire fences did more than this; they shut off the great trails that stretched from Corpus Christi through the Pan Handle of Texas, and on up through New Mexico and Colorado and through the Indian Territory to Dodge City. The coming of the railroad also made this trailing of cattle to the markets superfluous, and almost destroyed one of the most remarkable features of the West. This trail was not, of course, an actual trail, and marked as such, but a general driveway forty miles wide and thousands of miles long. The herds of cattle that were driven over it numbered from three hundred to three thousand head, and were moving constantly from the early spring to the late fall.

No caravan route in the far Eastern countries can equal this six months' journey through three different States, and through all changes of weather and climate, and in the

FIXING A BREAK IN THE WIRE FENCE

Ranch Life in Texas

face of constant danger and anxiety. This procession of countless cattle on their slow march to the north was one of the most interesting and distinctive features of the West.

An "outfit" for this expedition would consist of as many cowboys as were needed to hold the herd together, a wagon, with the cook and the tents, and extra ponies for the riders. In the morning the camp-wagon pushed on ahead to a suitable resting-place for the night, and when the herd arrived later, moving, on an average, fifteen miles a day, and grazing as it went, the men would find the supper ready and the tents pitched. And then those who were to watch that night would circle slowly around the great army of cattle, driving them in closer and closer together, and singing as they rode, to put them to sleep. This seems an absurdity to the Eastern mind, but the familiar sounds quieted and satisfied these great stupid animals that can be soothed like a child with a nursery rhyme, and when frightened cannot be stopped by a river. The boys rode slowly and patiently until one and then another of the herd would stumble clumsily to the ground, and others near would follow, and at last the whole great herd would be silent and immovable in sleep. But the watchfulness of the sentries could never relax. Some chance noise—the shaking of a saddle, some cry of a wild animal, or the scent of distant water carried by a chance breeze across the prairie, or nothing but sheer blind wantonness—would start one of the sleeping mass to his feet with a snort, and in an instant the whole great herd would go tearing madly over the prairie, tossing their horns and bellowing, and filled with a wild, unreasoning terror. And then the skill and daring of the cowboy was put to its severest test, as he saw his master's income disappearing towards a cañon or a river, or to lose itself in the brush. And the cowboy who tried to head off and drive back this galloping army of frantic animals had to ride a race that meant his life if his horse made a misstep; and as the horse's feet often did slip, there would be found in the morning somewhere in the trail of the stampeding cattle a horrid mass of blood and flesh and leather.

Do you wonder, then, after this half-year of weary, restless riding by day, and sleepless anxiety and watching under the stars by night, that when the lights of Dodge City showed across the prairie, the cowboy kicked his feet out of his stirrups, drove the blood out of the pony's sides, and "came in to town" with both guns going at once, and yelling as though the pent-up speech of the past six months of loneliness was striving for proper utterance?

The cowboy cannot be overestimated as a picturesque figure; all that has been written about him and all the illustrations that have been made of him fail to familiarize him, and to spoil the picture he makes when one sees him for the first time racing across a range outlined against the sky, with his handkerchief flying out behind, his sombrero bent back by the wind, and his gauntlets and broad leather leggings showing above and at the side of his galloping pony. And his deep seat in the saddle, with his legs hanging straight to the long stirrups, the movement of his body as it sways and bends, and his utter unconsciousness of the animal beneath him would make a German riding-master, an English jockey, or the best cross-country rider of a Long Island hunting club shake his head in envy and despair.

He is a fantastic-looking individual, and one suspects he wears the strange garments he affects because he knows they are most becoming. But there is a reason for each

GATHERING THE ROPE

of the different parts of his apparel, in spite of rather than on account of their picturesqueness. The sombrero shades his face from the rain and sun, the rattlesnake-skin around it keeps it on his head, the broad kerchief that he wears knotted around his throat protects his neck from the heat, and the leather leggings which cover the front of his legs protect them from the cactus in Texas, and in the North, where the fur and hair are left on the leather, from the sleet and rain as he rides against them. The gauntlets certainly seem too military for such rough service, but any one who has had a sheet rope run through his hands, can imagine how a lasso cuts when a wild horse is pulling on the other end of it. His cartridge-belt and his revolver are on some ranches superfluous, but cattle-men say they have found that on those days when they took this toy away from their boys, they sulked and fretted and went about their work half-heartedly, so that they believe it pays better to humor them, and to allow them to relieve the monotony of the day's vigil by popping at jack-rabbits and learning to twirl their revolver around their first finger. Of the many compliments I have heard paid by officers and privates and ranch-owners and cowboys to Mr. Frederic Remington, the one which was sure to follow the others was that he never made the mistake of putting the revolver on the left side. But as I went North, his anonymous admirers would make this same comment, but with regret that he should be guilty of such an error. I could not understand this at first until I found that the two sides of the shield lay in the Northern cowboy's custom of wearing his pistol on the left, and of the Texan's of carrying it on the right. The Northern man argues on this important matter that the sword has always been worn on the left, that it is easier to reach across and sweep the pistol to either the left or right, and that with this motion it is at once in position. The Texan says this is absurd, and quotes the fact that the pistol-pocket has always been on the right, and that the lasso and reins are in the way of the left hand. It is too grave a question of etiquette for any one who has not at least six notches on his pistol-butt to decide.

Although Mr. Kleberg's cowboys have been shorn of their pistols, their prowess as ropers still remains with them. They gave us an exhibition of this feature of their calling which was as remarkable a performance in its way as I have ever seen. The audience seated itself on the top of a seven-rail fence, and thrilled with excitement. At least a part of it did. I fancy Mr. Kleberg was slightly bored, but he was too polite to show it. Sixty wild horses were sent into a pen eighty yards across, and surrounded by the seven-rail fence. Into this the cowboys came, mounted on their ponies, and at Mr. Kleberg's word lassoed whichever horse he designated. They threw their ropes as a man tosses a quoit, drawing it back at the instant it closed over the horse's head, and not, as the beginner does, allowing the noose to settle loosely, and to tighten through the horse's effort to move forward. This roping was not so impressive as what followed, as the ropes were short, owing to the thick undergrowth, which prevents long throws, such as are made in the North, and as the pony was trained to suit its gait to that of the animal it was pursuing, and to turn and dodge with it, and to stop with both forefeet planted firmly when the rope had settled around the other horse's neck.

But when they had shown us how very simple a matter this was, they were told to dismount and to rope the horses

REACTION EQUALS ACTION

by whichever foot Mr. Kleberg choose to select. This was a real combat, and was as intensely interesting a contest between a thoroughly wild and terrified animal and a perfectly cool man as one can see, except, perhaps, at a bullfight. There is something in a contest of this sort that has appealed to something in all human beings who have blood in their veins from the days when one gladiator followed another with a casting-net and a trident around the arena down to the present, when "Peter" Poe drops on one knee and tries to throw Hefflefinger over his shoulder. In this the odds were in favor of the horse, as a cowboy on the ground is as much out of his element as a sailor on a horse, and looks as strangely. The boys moved and ran and backed away as quickly as their heavy leggings would permit; but the horses moved just twice as quickly, turning and jumping and rearing, and then racing away out of reach again at a gallop. But whenever they came within range of the ropes, they fell. The roping around the neck had seemed simple. The rope then was cast in a loop with a noose at one end as easily as one throws a trout line. But now the rope had to be hurled as quickly and as surely as a man sends a ball to first base when the batsman is running, except that the object at which the cowboy aims is moving at a gallop, and one of a galloping horse's four feet is a most uncertain bull's-eye.

It is almost impossible to describe the swiftness with which the rope moved. It seemed to skim across the ground as a skipping-rope does when a child holds one end of it and shakes the rope up and down to make it look like a snake coiling and undulating over the pavement.

One instant the rope would hang coiled from the thrower's right hand as he ran forward to meet the horse, moving it slowly, with a twist of his wrist, to keep it from snarling, and the next it would spin out along the ground, with the noose rolling like a hoop in the front, and would close with a snap over the horse's hoof, and the cowboy would throw himself back to take the shock, and the horse would come down on its side as though the ground had slipped from under it.

The roping around the neck was the easy tossing of a quoit; the roping around the leg was the angry snapping of a whip.

There are thousands of other ranches in the United States besides those in Texas, and other cowboys, but the general characteristics are the same in all, and it is only general characteristics that one can attempt to give.

VI

ON AN INDIAN RESERVATION

VI

ON AN INDIAN RESERVATION

THE American Indian may be considered either seriously or lightly, according to one's inclination and opportunities. He may be taken seriously, like the Irish question, by politicians and philanthropists; or lightly, as a picturesque and historic relic of the past, as one regards the beef-eaters, the Tower, or the fishwives at Scheveningen. There are a great many Indians and a great many reservations, and some are partly civilized and others are not, and the different tribes differ in speech and manner of life as widely as in the South the clay-eater of Alabama differs from a gentleman of one of the first families of Virginia. Any one who wishes to speak with authority on the American Indian must learn much more concerning him than the names of the tribes and the agencies.

The Indian will only be considered here lightly and as a picturesque figure of the West.

Many years ago the people of the East took their idea of the Indian from Cooper's novels and "Hiawatha," and pictured him shooting arrows into herds of buffalo, and sitting in his wigwam with many scalp-locks drying on his shield in the sun outside. But they know better than that now. Travellers from the West have told them that this picture

The West from a Car-Window

THE CHEYENNE TYPE

belongs to the past, and they have been taught to look upon the Indian as a "problem," and to consider him as either a national nuisance or as a much-cheated and ill-used brother. They think of him, if they think of him at all, as one who has fallen from his high estate, and who is a dirty individual hanging around agencies in a high hat and a red shirt with a whiskey-bottle under his arm, waiting a chance

On an Indian Reservation

to beg or steal. The Indian I saw was not at all like this, but was still picturesque, not only in what he wore, but in what he did and said, and was full of a dignity that came up at unexpected moments, and was as suspicious or trustful as a child.

It is impossible when one sees a blanket Indian walking haughtily about in his buckskin, with his face painted in many colors and with feathers in his hair, not to think that he has dressed for the occasion, or goes thus equipped because his forefathers did so, and not because he finds it comfortable. When you have seen a particular national costume only in pictures and photographs, it is always something of a surprise to find people wearing it with every-day matter-of-course ease, as though they really preferred kilts or sabots or moccasins to the gear to which we are accustomed at home. And the Indians in their fantastic mixture of colors and beads and red flannel and feathers seemed so theatrical at first that I could not understand why the army officers did not look back over their shoulders when one of these young braves rode by. The first Indians I saw were at Fort Reno, where there is an agency for the Cheyennes and Arapahoes. This reservation is in the Oklahoma Territory, but the Government has bought it from the Indians for a half-dollar an acre, and it is to be opened to white settlers. The country is very beautiful, and the tall grass of the prairie, which hides a pony, and shows only the red blanketed figure on his back, and over which in the clear places the little prairie-dogs scamper, and where the red buttes stand out against the sky, and show an edge as sharp and curving as the prow of a man-of-war, gives one a view of a West one seems to have visited and known intimately through the illustrated papers.

The West from a Car-Window

I had gone to Fort Reno to see the beef issue which takes place there every two weeks, when the steers and the other things which make up the Indian's rations are distributed by the agent. I missed the issue by four hours, and had to push on to Anadarko, where another beef issue was to come off three days later, which was trying, as I had met few men more interesting and delightful than the officers at the post-trader's mess. But I was fortunate, in the short time in which I was at Fort Reno, in stumbling upon an Indian council. Two lieutenants and a surgeon and I had ridden over to the Indian agency, and although they allow no beer on an Indian reservation, the surgeon had hopes. It had been a long ride—partly through water, partly over a dusty trail—and it was hot. But if the agent had a private store for visitors, he was not in a position to offer it, for his room was crowded with chiefs of renown and high degree. They sat in a circle around his desk on the floor, or stood against the wall smoking solemnly. When they approved of what the speaker said, they grunted; and though that is the only word for it, they somehow made that form of "hear, hear," impressive. Those chiefs who spoke talked in a spitting, guttural fashion, far down the throat, and without gestures; and the son of one of them, a boy from Carlisle, in a gray ready-made suit and sombrero, translated a five-minutes' speech, which had all the dignity of Salvini's address to the Senators, by: "And Red Wolf he says he thinks it isn't right." Cloud-Shield rose and said the chiefs were glad to see that the officers from the fort were in the room, as that meant that the Indian would have fair treatment, and that the officers were always the Indians' best friends, and were respected in times of peace as friends, and in times of war as enemies.

On an Indian Reservation

After which, the officers, considering guiltily the real object of their visit, and feeling properly abashed, took off their hats and tried to look as though they deserved it, which, as a rule, they do. It may be of interest, in view of an Indian outbreak, to know that this council of the chiefs was to protest against the cutting down of the rations of the Cheyennes and the Arapahoes. Last year it cost the Government one hundred and thirteen thousand dollars to feed them, and this year Commissioner Martin, with a fine spirit of economy, proposes to reduce this by just one-half. This means hunger and illness, and in some cases death.

"He says," translated the boy interpreter, gazing at the ceiling, "that they would like to speak to the people at Washington about this thing, for it is not good."

The agent traced figures over his desk with his pen.

"Well, I can't do anything," he said, at last. "All I can do is to let the people at Washington know what they say. But to send a commission all the way to Washington will take a great deal of money, and the cost of it will have to come out of their allowance. Tell them that. Tell them I'll write on about it. That's all I can do."

That night the chiefs came solemnly across parade, and said "How!" grimly to the orderly in front of the colonel's headquarters.

"You see," said the officers, "they have come to complain, but the colonel cannot help them. If Martin wants a war, he is going just the best way in the world to get it, and then we shall have to go out and shoot them, poor devils!"

I was very sorry to leave Fort Reno, not only on account of the officers there, but because the ride to Anadarko must be made in stages owned by a Mr. Williamson. This is not intended as an advertisement for Mr. Williamson's stages. He does not need it, for he is, so his drivers tell me, very rich indeed, and so economical that he makes them buy their own whips. Every one who has travelled through the Indian Territory over Mr. Williamson's routes wishes that sad things may happen to him; but no one, I believe, would be so wicked as to hope he may ever have to ride in one of his own stages. The stage-coach of the Indian Territory lacks the romance of those that Dick Turpin stopped, or of the Deadwood coach, or of those that Yuba Bill drives for Bret Harte with four horses, with gamblers on top and road-agents at the horses' heads. They are only low four-wheeled wagons with canvas sides and top, and each revolution of the wheels seems to loosen every stick and nail, and throws you sometimes on top of the driver, and sometimes the driver on top of you. They hold together, though, and float bravely through creeks, and spin down the side of a cañon on one wheel, and toil up the other side on two, and at such an angle that you see the sun bisected by the wagon-tongue. At night the stage seems to plunge a little more than in the day, and you spend it in trying to sleep with your legs under the back seat and your head on the one in front, while the driver, who wants to sleep and cannot, shouts profanely to his mules and very near to your ear on the other side of the canvas.

Anadarko is a town of six stores, three or four frame houses, the Indian agent's store and office, and the City Hotel. Seven houses in the West make a city. I said I thought this was the worst hotel in the Indian Territory, but the officers at Fort Sill, who have travelled more than I, think it is the worst in the United States. It is possible that they are right. There are bluffs and bunches of timber

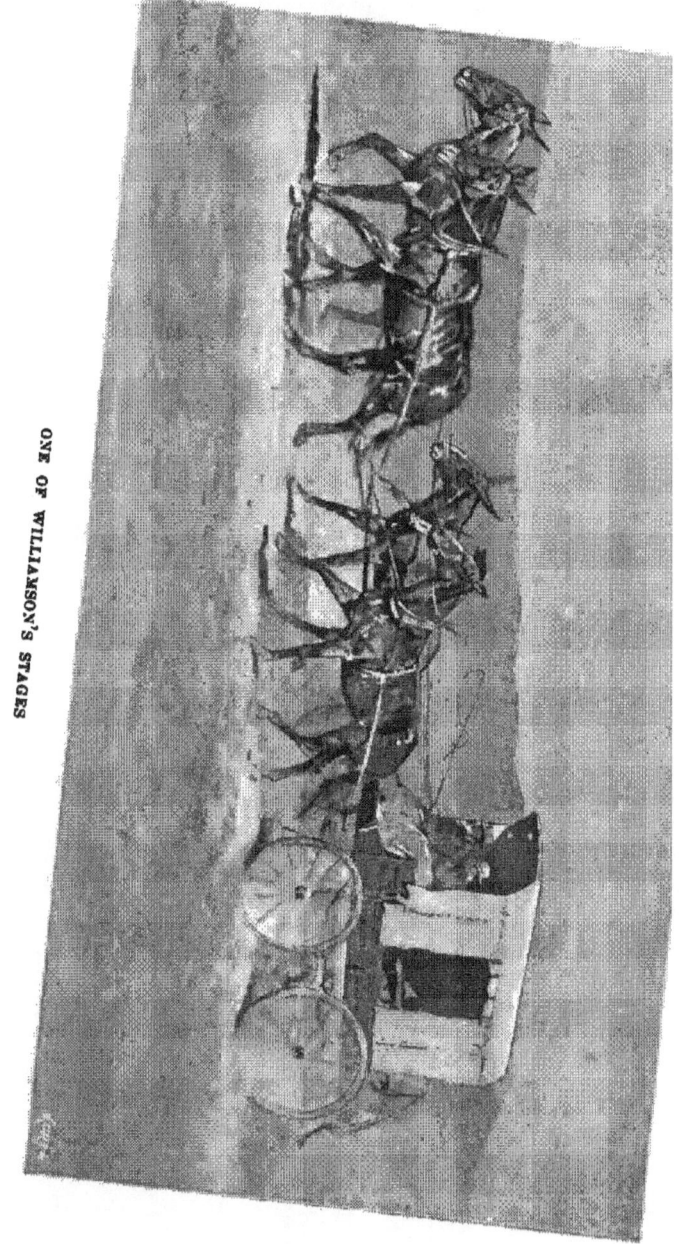

ONE OF WILLIAMSON'S STAGES

On an Indian Reservation

around Anadarko, but the prairie stretches towards the west, and on it is the pen from which the cattle are issued. The tepees and camp-fires sprang up overnight, and when we came out the next morning the prairie was crowded with them, and more Indians were driving in every minute, with the family in the wagon and the dogs under it, as the country people in the East flock into town for the circus. The men galloped off to the cattle-pen, and the women gathered in a long line in front of the agent's store to wait their turn for the rations. It was a curious line, with very young girls in it, very proud of the little babies in beaded knapsacks on their backs—dirty, bright-eyed babies that looked like mummies suddenly come to life again at the period of their first childhood—and wrinkled, bent old squaws, even more like mummies, with coarse white hair, and hands worn almost out of shape with work. Each of these had a tag, such as those that the express companies use, on which was printed the number in each family, and the amount of grain, flour, baking-powder, and soap to which the family was entitled. They passed in at one door and in front of a long counter, and out at another. They crowded and pushed a great deal, almost as much as their fairer sisters do in front of the box-office at a Patti matinée, and the babies blinked stoically at the sun, and seemed to wish they could get their arms out of the wrappings and rub away the tears. A man in a sombrero would look at the tag and call out, "One of flour, two of sugar, one soap, and one baking-powder," and his Indian assistants delved into the barrels behind the line of the counter, and emptied the rations into the squaw's open apron. She sorted them when she reached the outside. By ten o'clock the distribution was over, and the women followed the men to the cattle-pen on the prairie. There were not over three hundred Indians there, although they represented several thousand others, who remained in the different camps scattered over the reservation, wherever water and timber, and bluffs to shield them best from the wind, were to be found in common. Each steer is calculated to supply twenty-five Indians with beef for two weeks, or from one and a half to two pounds of beef a day; this is on the supposition that the steers average from one thousand to one thousand and two hundred pounds. The steers that I saw issued weighed about five hundred pounds, and when they tried to run, stumbled with the weakness of starvation. They were nothing but hide and ribs and two horns. They were driven four at a time through a long chute, and halted at the gate at the end of it until their owner's names were marked off the list. The Indians were gathered in front of the gate in long rows, or in groups of ten or twelve, sitting easily in their saddles, and riding off leisurely in bunches of four as their names were called out, and as their cattle were started off with a parting kick into the open prairie.

The Apaches, Comanches, Delawares, and Towacomies drove their share off towards their camps; the Caddoes and the Kiowas, who live near the agency, and who were served last, killed theirs, if they chose to do so, as soon as they left the pen. A man in charge of the issue held a long paper in his hand, and called out, "Eck-hoos-cho, Pe-an-voon-it, Hoos-cho, and Cho-noo-chy," which meant that Red-Bird, Large-Looking-Glass, The Bird, and Deer-Head were to have the next four steers. His assistant, an Indian policeman, with "God helps them who help themselves" engraved on his brass buttons, with the figure of an Indian toiling at a plough in the centre, repeated these

THE BEEF ISSUE AT ANADARKO

On an Indian Reservation

names aloud, and designated which steer was to go to which Indian.

A beef issue is not a pretty thing to watch. Why the Government does not serve its meat with the throats cut, as any reputable butcher would do, it is not possible to determine. It seems to prefer, on the contrary, that the Indian should exhibit his disregard for the suffering of animals and his bad marksmanship at the same time. When the representatives of the more distant tribes had ridden off, chasing their beef before them, the Caddoes and Kiowas gathered close around the gate of the pen, with the boys in front. They were handsome, mischievous boys, with leather leggings, colored green and blue and with silver buttons down the side, and beaded buckskin shirts. They sat two on each pony, and each held his bow and arrows, and as the steers came stumbling blindly out into the open, they let the arrows drive from a distance of ten feet into the animal's flank and neck, where they stuck quivering. Then the Indian boys would yell, and their fathers, who had hunted buffaloes with arrows, smiled approvingly. The arrows were not big enough to kill, they merely hurt, and the steer would rush off into a clumsy gallop for fifty yards, when its owner would raise his Winchester, and make the dust spurt up around, it until one bullet would reach a leg, and the steer would stop for an instant, with a desperate toss of its head, and stagger forward again on three. The dogs to the number of twenty or more were around it by this time in a snarling, leaping pack, and the owner would try again, and wound it perhaps in the flank, and it would lurch over heavily like a drunken man, shaking its head from side to side and tossing its horns at the dogs, who bit at the place where the blood ran, and snapped at its legs. Sometimes it would lie there for an hour, until it bled to death, or, again, it would scramble to its feet, and the dogs would start off in a panic of fear after a more helpless victim.

The field grew thick with these miniature butcheries, the Winchesters cracking, and the spurts of smoke rising and drifting away, the dogs yelping, and the Indians wheeling in quick circles around the steer, shooting as they rode, and hitting the mark once in every half-dozen shots. It was the most unsportsmanlike and wantonly cruel exhibition I have ever seen. A bull in a ring has a fighting chance and takes it, but these animals, who were too weak to stand, and too frightened to run, staggered about until the Indians had finished torturing them, and then, with eyes rolling and blood spurting from their mouths, would pitch forward and die. And they had to be quick about it, before the squaws began cutting off the hide while the flanks were still heaving.

This is the view of a beef issue which the friend of the Indian does not like to take. He prefers calling your attention to the condition of the cattle served the Indian, and in showing how outrageously he is treated in this respect. The Government either purchases steers for the Indians a few weeks before an issue, or three or four months previous to it, feeding them meanwhile on the Government reservation. The latter practice is much more satisfactory to the contractor, as it saves him the cost and care of these cattle during the winter, and the inevitable loss which must ensue in that time through illness and starvation. Those I saw had been purchased in October, and had been weighed and branded at that time with the Government brand. They were then allowed to roam over the Government reservation

On an Indian Reservation

until the spring, when they had fallen off in weight from one-half to one-third. They were then issued at their original weight. That is, a steer which in October was found to weigh eleven hundred pounds, and which would supply twenty or more people with meat, was supposed to have kept this weight throughout the entire winter, and was issued at eleven hundred although it had not three hundred pounds of flesh on its bones. The agent is not to blame for this. This is the fault of the Government, and it is quite fair to suppose that some one besides the contractor benefits by the arrangement. When the beef is issued two weeks after the contract has been made, it can and frequently is rejected by the army officer in charge of the issue if he thinks it is unfit. But the officers present at the issue that I saw were as helpless as they were indignant, for the beef had weighed the weight credited to it once when it was paid for, and the contractor had saved the expense of keeping it, and the Indian received just one-fourth of the meat due him, and for which he had paid in land.

Fort Sill, which is a day's journey in a stage from Anadarko, is an eight-company post situated on the table-land of a hill, with other hills around it, and is, though somewhat inaccessible, as interesting and beautiful a spot to visit as many others which we cross the ocean to see. I will be able to tell why this is so when I write something later about the army posts. There are any number of Indians here, and they add to the post a delightfully picturesque and foreign element. L Troop of the Seventh cavalry, which is an Indian troop, is the nucleus around which the other Indians gather. The troop is encamped at the foot of the hill on which the post stands. It shows the Indian civilized by uniform, and his Indian brother uncivilized in his blanket and war-paint; and although I should not like to hurt the feelings of the patient, enthusiastic officers who have enlisted the Indians for these different troops for which the Government calls, I think the blanket Indian is a much more warlike-looking and interesting individual. But you mustn't say so, as George the Third advised. The soldier Indians live in regulation tents staked out in rows, and with the ground around so cleanly kept that one could play tennis on it, and immediately back of these are the conical tepees of their wives, brothers, and grandmothers; and what Lieutenant Scott is going to do with all these pretty young squaws and beautiful children and withered old witches, and their two or three hundred wolf-dogs, when he marches forth to war with his Indian troop, is one of the questions his brother officers find much entertainment in asking.

The Indian children around this encampment were the brightest spot in my entire Western trip. They are the prettiest and most beautifully barbaric little children I have ever seen. They grow out of it very soon, but that is no reason why one should not make the most of it while it lasts. And they are as wild and fearful of the white visitor, unless he happens to be Lieutenant Scott or Second Lieutenant Quay, as the antelope in the prairie around him. It required a corporal's guard, two lieutenants, and three squaws to persuade one of them to stand still and be photographed, and whenever my camera and I appeared together there was a wild stampede of Indian children, which no number of looking-glasses or dimes or strings of beads could allay. Not that they would not take the bribes, but they would run as soon as they had snatched them. It was very distressing, for I did not mean to hurt them very much.

INDIAN BOY AND PINTO PONY

On an Indian Reservation

The older people were kinder, and would let me sit inside the tepees, which were very warm on the coldest days, and watch them cook, and play their queer games, and work moccasins, and gamble at monte for brass rings if they were women, or for cartridges if they were men. And for ways that are dark and tricks that are vain, I think the Indian monte-dealer can instruct a Chinese poker-player in many things. What was so fine about them was their dignity, hospitality, and strict suppression of all curiosity. They always received a present as though they were doing you a favor, and you felt that you were paying tribute. This makes them difficult to deal with as soldiers. They cannot be treated as white men, and put in the guard-house for every slight offence. Lieutenant Scott has to explain things to them, and praise them, and excite a spirit of emulation among them by commending those publicly who have done well. For instance, they hate to lose their long hair, and Lieutenant Scott did not order them to have it cut, but told them it would please him if they did; and so one by one, and in bunches of three and four, they tramped up the hill to the post barber, and back again with their locks in their hands, to barter them for tobacco with the post trader. The Indians at Fort Sill were a temperate lot, and Lieutenant Harris, who has charge of the canteen, growled because they did not drink enough to pay for their share of the dividend which is returned to each troop at the end of the month.

Lieutenant Scott obtained his ascendency over his troop in several ways — first, by climbing a face of rock, and, with the assistance of Lieutenant Quay, taking an eagle from the nest it had built there. Every Indian in the reservation knew of that nest, and had long wanted the eagle's feathers for a war-bonnet, but none of them had ever dared to climb the mirrorlike surface of the cliff, with the rocks below. The fame of this exploit spread, by what means it is hard to understand among people who have no newspapers or letters, but at beef issues, perhaps, or Messiah dances, or casual meetings on the prairie, which help to build up reputations and make the prowess of one chief known to those of all the other tribes, or the beauty of an Indian girl familiar. Then, following this exploit, three little Indian children ran away from school because they had been flogged, and tried to reach their father's tent fifteen miles off on the reservation, and were found half-buried in the snow and frozen to death. One of them was without his heavier garments, which he had wrapped around his younger brother. The terrified school-teacher sent a message to the fort begging for two troops of cavalry to protect him from the wrath of the older Indians, and the post commander sent out Lieutenant Scott alone to treat with them. His words were much more effective than two troops of cavalry would have been, and the threatened outbreak was stopped. The school-master fled to the woods, and never came back. What the Indians saw of Lieutenant Scott at this crisis made them trust him for the future, and this and the robbery of the eagle's nest explain partly, as do his gentleness and consideration, the remarkable hold he has over them. Some one was trying to tell one of the chiefs how the white man could bring lightning down from the sky, and make it talk for him from one end of the country to the other.

"Oh yes," the Indian said, simply, "that is quite true. Lieutenant Scott says so."

But what has chiefly contributed to make the lieuten-

On an Indian Reservation

ant's work easy for him is his knowledge of the sign language, with which the different tribes, though speaking different languages, can communicate one with the other. He is said to speak this more correctly and fluently than any other officer in the army, and perhaps any other white man. It is a very curious language. It is not at all like the deaf-and-dumb alphabet, which *is* an alphabet, and is not pretty to watch. It is just what its name implies—a language of signs. The first time I saw the lieutenant speaking it, I confess I thought, having heard of his skill at Fort Reno, that he was only doing it because he could do it, as young men who speak French prefer to order their American dinners in that language when the waiter can understand English quite as well as themselves. I regarded it as a pleasing weakness, and was quite sure that the lieutenant was going to meet the Indian back of the canteen and say it over again in plain every-day words. In this I wronged him; but it was not until I had watched his Irish sergeant converse in this silent language for two long hours with half a dozen Indians of different tribes, and had seen them all laugh heartily at his witticisms delivered in semaphoric gestures, that I really believed in it. It seems that what the lieutenant said was, "Tell the first sergeant that I wish to see the soldiers drill at one o'clock, and, after that, go to the store and ask Madeira if there is to be a beef issue to-day." It is very difficult to describe in writing how he did this; and as it is a really pretty thing to watch, it seems a pity to spoil it. As well as I remember it, he did something like this. He first drew his hand over his sleeve to mark the sergeant's stripes; then he held his fingers upright in front of him, and moved them forward to signify soldiers; by holding them in still another position, he represented soldiers drilling; then he made a spyglass out of his thumb and first finger, and looked up through it at the sky — this represented the sun at one o'clock. "After that" was a quick cut in the air; the "store" was an interlacing of the fingers, to signify a place where one thing met or was exchanged for another; "Madeira" he named; beef was a turning up of the fingers, to represent horns; and how he represented issue I have no idea. It is a most curious thing to watch, for they change from one sign to the other with the greatest rapidity. I always regarded it with great interest as a sort of game, and tried to guess what the different gestures might mean. Some of the signs are very old, and their origin is as much in dispute as some of the lines in the first folios of Shakespeare, and have nearly as many commentators. All the Indians know these signs, but very few of them can tell how they came to mean what they do. "To go to war," for instance, is shown by sweeping the right arm out with the thumb and first finger at right angles; this comes from an early custom among the Indians of carrying a lighted pipe before them when going on the war-path. The thumb and finger in that position are supposed to represent the angle of the bowl of the pipe and the stem.

I visited a few of the Indian schools when I was in the Territory, and found the pupils quite learned. The teachers are not permitted to study the Indian languages, and their charges in consequence hear nothing but English, and so pick it up the more quickly. The young women who teach them seem to labor under certain disadvantages; one of them was reading the English lesson from a United States history intended for much older children — grown-up children, in fact — and explained that she had to order and

A KIOWA MAIDEN

select the school-books she used from a list furnished by the Government, and could form no opinion of its appropriateness until it arrived.

Some of the Indian parents are very proud of their children's progress, and on beef-issue days visit the schools, and listen with great satisfaction to their children speaking in the unknown tongue. There were several in one of the school-rooms while I was there, and the teacher turned them out of their chairs to make room for us, remarking pleasantly that the Indians were accustomed to sitting around on the ground. She afterwards added to this by telling us that there was no sentiment in *her*, and that she taught Indians for the fifty dollars there was in it. The mother of one of the little boys was already crouching on the floor as we came in, or squatting on her heels, as they seem to be able to do without fatigue for any length of time. During the half-hour we were there, she never changed her position or turned her head to look at us, but kept her eyes fixed only on her son sitting on the bench above her. He was a very plump, clean, and excited little Indian, with his hair cut short, and dressed in a very fine pair of trousers and jacket, and with shoes and stockings. He was very keen to show the white visitors how well he knew their talk, and read his book with a masterful shaking of the head, as though it had no terrors for him. His mother, kneeling at his side on the floor, wore a single garment, and over that a dirty blanket strapped around her waist with a beaded belt. Her feet were bare, and her coarse hair hung down over her face and down her back almost to her waist in an unkempt mass. She supported her chin on one hand, and with the other hand, black and wrinkled, and with nails broken by cutting wood and harnessing horses and ploughing in the fields, brushed her hair back from before her eyes, and then touched her son's arm wistfully, as a dog tries to draw his master's eyes, and as though he were something fragile and fine. But he paid no attention to her whatsoever; he was very much interested in the lesson. She was the only thing I saw in the school-room. I wondered if she was thinking of the days when she carried his weight on her back as she went about her cooking or foraging for wood, or swung him from a limb of a tree, and of the first leather leggings she made for him when he was able to walk, and of the necklace of elk teeth, and the arrows which he used to fire bravely at the prairie-dogs. He was a very different child now, and very far away from the doglike figure crouching by his side and gazing up patiently into his face, as if looking for something she had lost.

It is quite too presumptuous to suggest any opinion on the Indian question when one has only lived with them for three weeks, but the experience of others who have lived with them for thirty years is worth repeating. You will find that the individual point of view regarding the Indian is much biassed by the individual interests. A man told me that in his eyes no one under heaven was better than a white man, and if the white man had to work for his living, he could not see why the Indian should not work for his. I asked him if he thought of taking up Indian land in the Territory when it was open in the spring, and he said that was his intention, "and why?"

The officers are the only men who have absolutely nothing to gain, make, or lose by the Indians, and their point of view is accordingly the fairest, and they themselves say it would be a mistake to follow the plan now under consideration—of placing officers in charge of the agencies. This would at once strip them of their present neutral position, and, as well, open to them the temptation which the control of many thousands of dollars' worth of property entails where the recipients of this property are as helpless and ignorant as children. They rather favor raising the salary of the Indian agent from two thousand to ten thousand dollars, and by so doing bring men of intelligence and probity into the service, and destroy at the same time the temptation to "make something" out of the office. It may have been merely an accident, but I did not meet with one officer in any of the army posts who did not side with the Indian in his battle for his rights with the Government. As for the agents, as the people say in the West, "they are not here for their health." The Indian agents of the present day are, as every one knows, political appointments, and many of them—not all—are men who at home would keep their corner grocery or liquor store, and who would flatter and be civil to every woman in the neighboring tenement who came for a pound of sugar or a pitcher of beer. These men are suddenly placed in the control of hundreds of sensitive, dangerous, semi-civilized people, whom they are as capable of understanding as a Bowery boy would be of appreciating an Arab of the desert.

The agents are not the only people who make mistakes. Some friend mailed me a book the other day on Indian reservations, in order that I might avoid writing what has already been written. I read only one page of the book, in which the author described his manner of visiting the Indian encampments. He would drive to one of these in his ambulance, and upon being informed that the chiefs were waiting to receive him in their tents, would bid them meet him at the next camp, to which he would drive rapidly, and there make the same proposition. He would then stop his wagon three miles away on the prairie, and wait for the chiefs to follow him to that point. What his object was in this exhibition, with which he seemed very well satisfied, he only knows. Whether it was to teach the chiefs they were not masters in their own camps, or that he was a most superior person, I could not make out; but he might just as effectively have visited Washington, and sent the President word he could not visit him at the White House, but that he would grant him an interview at his hotel. I wonder just how near this superior young man got to the Indians, and just how wide they opened their hearts to him.

There was an Indian agent once — it was not long ago, but there is no need to give dates or names, for the man is dead—who when the Indians asked him to paint the wagons (with which the Government furnished them through him in return for their land) red instead of green, answered that he would not pander to their absurdly barbaric tastes. Only he did not say absurdly. He was a man who had his own ideas about things, and who was not to be fooled, and he was also a superior person, who preferred to trample on rather than to understand the peculiarities of his wards. So one morning this agent and his wife and children were found hacked to pieces by these wards with barbaric tastes, and the soldiers were called out, and shot many of the Indians; and many white women back of the barracks, and on the line itself, are now wearing mourning, and several officers got their first bar. It would seem from this very recent incident, as well as from many others of which one hears, that it would be cheaper in the end to place agents over the Indians with sufficient intelligence to know just when to be firm, and when to compromise in a matter; for instance, that of painting a wagon red.

VII

A CIVILIAN AT AN ARMY POST

VII

A CIVILIAN AT AN ARMY POST

THE army posts of the United States are as different one from another as the stations along the line of a great railroad system. There is the same organization for all, and the highest officers govern one as well as the other; but in appearance and degree of usefulness and local rule they are as independent and yet as dependent, and as far apart in actual miles, as the Grand Central Depot in New York, with its twenty tracks and as many ticket-windows and oak-bound offices and greatest after-dinner orator, is distant from the section-house at the unfinished end of a road somewhere on the prairie. The commanding officer's quarters alone at Fort Sheridan cost thirty thousand dollars, and more than a million and a half has been spent on Fort Riley; but there are many other posts where nature supplied the mud and logs for the whole station, and the cost to the Government could not have been more than three hundred dollars at the most. It is consequently difficult to write in a general way of army posts. What is true of one is by no means true of another, and it will be better, perhaps, to first tell of those army posts which possess many features in common — eight-company posts, for instance, which are not too large nor too small, not too near civilization, and yet not too far removed from the railroad. An eight-company post is a little town or community of about three hundred people living in a quadrangle around a parade-ground. The scenery surrounding the quadrangle may differ as widely as you please to imagine it; it may be mountainous and beautiful, or level, flat, and unprofitable, but the parade-ground is always the same. It has a flag-pole at the entrance to the quadrangle, and a base-ball diamond marked out on the side on which the men live, and tennis-courts towards the officers' quarters. When you speak of the side of the square where the enlisted men live, you say "barracks," and you refer to the officers' share of the quadrangle as "the line." In England you can safely say that an officer is living in barracks, but you must not say this of a United States officer; he lives in the third or fourth house up or down "the line."

The barracks are a long continuous row of single-story buildings with covered porches facing the parade. They are generally painted an uncompromising brown, and are much more beautiful inside than out, especially the mess-rooms, where all the wood-work has been scrubbed so hard that the tables are worn almost to a concave surface. The architectural appearance of the officers' quarters on the line differs in different posts; but each house of each individual post, whether it is a double or single house, is alike to the number of bricks in the walls and in the exact arrangement of the rooms. The wives of the officers may change the outer appearance of their homes by planting rose-bushes and ivy about the yards, but whenever they do, some other officer's wife is immediately transferred from another post and "outranks" them, and they have to move farther down the line, and watch the new-comer plucking *their* roses, and

A ONE-COMPANY POST AT OKLAHOMA CITY

A Civilian at an Army Post

reaping the harvest she has not sown. This rule also applies to new wall-paper, and the introduction at your own expense of open fireplaces, with blue and white tiles which will not come off or out when the new-comer moves in. In addition to the officers' quarters and the barracks, there is an administration building, which is the executive mansion of this little community, a quartermaster's storehouse, a guard-house, and the hospital. The stables are back of the barracks, out of sight of those who live facing the parade, and there is generally a rear-guard of little huts and houses occupied by sergeants' wives, who do the washing for the posts, and do it very well. This is, briefly, the actual appearance of an army post—a quadrangle of houses, continuous and one-story high on two sides, and separate and two stories high on the other two sides, facing the parade, and occasionally surrounded by beautiful country.

The life of an army post, its internal arrangements, its necessary routine, and its expedients for breaking this routine pleasantly, cannot be dealt with so briefly; it is a delicate and extensive subject. It is impossible to separate the official and social life of an army post. The commanding officer does not lose that dignity which doth hedge him in when he and his orderly move from the administration building to his quarters, and it would obviously confuse matters if a second lieutenant bet him in the morning he could not put the red ball into the right-corner pocket, and in the evening at dress parade he should order the same lieutenant and his company into the lower right-hand corner of the parade at double-quick. This would tend to destroy discipline. And so, as far as the men of the post are concerned, the official and social life touch at many points. With the women, of course, it is different, although there was a colonel's wife not long ago who said to the officers' wives assisting her to receive at a dance, " You will take your places, ladies, in order of rank." I repeat this mild piece of gossip because it was the only piece of gossip I heard at any army post, which is interesting when one remembers the reputation given the army posts by one of their own people for that sort of thing.

The official head of the post is the commanding officer. He has under him eight " companies," if they are infantry, or " troops " if they are cavalry, each commanded in turn by a captain, who has under him a first and second lieutenant, who rule in their turn numerous sergeants and corporals. There is also a major or two, two or three surgeons, who rank with the captains, and a quartermaster and an adjutant, who are selected from among the captains or lieutenants of the post, and who perform, in consequence, double duty. The majority of the officers are married ; this is not a departmental regulation nor a general order, but it happens to be so. I visited one very large post in which every one was married except one girl, and a second lieutenant, who spoiled the natural sequel by being engaged to a girl somewhere else. And at the post I had visited before this there were ten unmarried and unengaged lieutenants, and no young women. It seems to me that this presents an unbalanced condition of affairs, which should be considered and adjusted by Congress even before the question of lineal promotion.

It is true that the commanding officer is supposed to be the most important personage in an army post, but that is not so. He, as well as every one else in it, is ruled by a young person with a brass trumpet, who apparently never sleeps, eats, or rests, and who spends his days tooting on his

THE OMNIPOTENT BUGLER

bugle in the middle of the parade in rainy and in sunny weather and through good and evil report. He sounds in all thirty-seven "calls" a day, and the garrison gets up and lies down, and eats, and waters the horses, and goes to church and school, and to horse exercise, and mounts guard, and drills recruits, and parades in full dress whenever he thinks they should. His prettiest call is reveille, which is sounded at half-past six in the morning. It is bright and spirited, and breathes promise and hope for the new day, and I personally liked it best because it meant that while I still had an hour to sleep, three hundred other men had to get up and clean cold guns and things in the semi-darkness. Next to the bugler in importance is the quartermaster. He is a captain or a first lieutenant with rare executive ability, and it is he who supplies the garrison with those things which make life bearable or luxurious, and it is he who is responsible to the Government for every coat of whitewash on the stables, and for the new stove-lid furnished the cook of N Troop, Thirteenth Cavalry. He is the hardest-worked man in the post, although that would possibly be denied by every other officer in it; and he is supposed to be an authority on architecture, sanitary plumbing, veterinary surgery, household furnishing from the kitchen range to the electric button on the front door, and to know all things concerning martial equipments from a sling-belt to an ambulance.

He is a wonderful man, and possessed of a vast and intricate knowledge, but his position in the post is very much like that of a base-ball umpire's on the field, for he is never thanked if he does well, and is abused by every one on principle. And he is never free. At the very minute he is lifting the green mint to his lips, his host will say, "By-the-way, my striker tells me that last piece of stove-pipe you furnished us does not fit by two inches; I don't believe you looked at the dimensions;" and when he hastens to join the ladies for protection, he is saluted with an anxious chorus of inquiries as to when he is going to put that pane of glass in the second-story window, and where are those bricks for the new chimney. His worst enemies, however, lie far afield, for he wages constant war with those clerks at the Treasury Department at Washington who go over his accounts and papers, and who take keen and justifiable pride in making him answer for every fraction of a cent which he has left unexplained. The Government, for instance, furnishes his storehouse with a thousand boxes of baking-powder, valued at seventy dollars, or seven cents a box. If he sells three boxes for twenty-five cents—I am quoting an actual instance—the Treasury Department returns his papers, requesting him to explain who got the four cents, and is anxious to know what he means by it.

I once saw some tin roofs at a post; they had been broken in coming, and the quartermaster condemned them. That was a year ago, and his papers complaining about these tin roofs have been travelling back and forth between contractor and express agent and the department at Washington and the quartermaster ever since, and they now make up a bundle of *seventy* different papers. Sometimes the quartermaster defeats the Treasury Department; sometimes it requires him to pay money out of his own pocket. Three revolvers were stolen out of their rack once, and the post quartermaster was held responsible for their loss. He objected to paying the sum the Government required, and pointed out that the revolvers should have been properly locked in the rack. The Government replied that the lock furnished by it was perfect, and not to be tampered with or

UNITED STATES MILITARY POST AT SAN ANTONIO

scoffed at, and that his excuse was puerile. This quartermaster had a mechanic in his company, and he sent for the young man, and told him to go through the barracks and open all the locks he could. At the end of an hour every rack and soldier's box in the post were burglarized, and the Government paid for the revolvers.

The post quartermaster's only pleasure lies in his storehouse, and in the neatness and order in which he keeps his supplies. He dearly loves to lead the civilian visitor through these long rows of shelves, and say, while clutching at his elbow to prevent his escape, "You see, there are all the shovels in that corner; then over there I have the Sibley tents, and there on that shelf are the blouses, and next to them are the overcoats, and there are the canvas shoes, and on that shelf we keep matches, and down here, you see, are the boots. Everything is in its proper place." At which you are to look interested, and say, "Ah, yes!" just as though you had expected to see the baking-powder mixed with the pith helmets, and the axe-handles and smoking-tobacco grouped together on the floor.

After the quartermaster, the adjutant, to the mind of the civilian at least, is the most superior being in the post. He is a lieutenant selected by the colonel to act as his conscience-keeper and letter-writer, and to convey his commands to the other officers. It is his proud privilege to sit in the colonel's own room and sign papers, and to dictate others to his assistant non-coms, and it is one of his duties to oversee the guard-mount, and to pick out the smartest-looking soldier to act as the colonel's orderly for the day. You must understand that as the colonel's orderly does not have to remain on guard at night, the men detailed for guard duty vie with each other in presenting an appearance sufficiently brilliant to attract the adjutant's eye, and as they all look exactly alike, the adjutant has to be careful. He sometimes spends five long minutes and much mental effort in going from one end of the ranks to the other to see if Number Three's boots are better blacked than Number Two's, and in trying to decide whether the fact that Murphy's gun-barrel is oilier than Cronin's should weigh against the fact that Cronin's gloves are new, while Murphy's are only fresh from the wash, both having tied on the condition of their cartridges, which have been rubbed to look like silver, and which must be an entirely superflous nicety to the Indian who may eventually be shot with them. This is one of the severest duties of an adjutant's routine, and after having accompanied one of them through one of these prize exhibitions, I was relieved to hear him confess his defeat by telling the sergeant that Cronin and Murphy could toss for it. Another perquisite of the adjutant's is his right to tell his brother officers at mess in a casual way that they must act as officer of the day or officer of the guard, or relieve Lieutenant Quay while he goes quail-hunting, or take charge of Captain Blank's troop of raw recruits until the captain returns to their relief. To be able to do this to men who outrank you, and who are much older than yourself, and just as though the orders came from you direct, must be a great pleasure, especially as the others are not allowed the satisfaction of asking, "Who says I must?" or, "What's the matter with your doing it yourself?" These are the officials of the post; the unofficials, the wives and the children, make the social life whatever it is.

There are many in the East who think life at an army post is one of discomfort and more or less monotony, relieved by petty gossip and flirtations. Of course one cannot

UNITED STATES CAVALRYMAN IN FULL DRESS

A Civilian at an Army Post

tell in a short visit whether or not the life might become monotonous, though one rather suspects it would, but the discomforts are quite balanced by other things which we cannot get in the city. Of jealousy and gossip I saw little. I was told by one officer's wife that to the railroads was due the credit of the destruction of flirtations at garrisons; and though I had heard of many great advances and changes of conditions and territories brought about by the coming of the railroads, this was the first time I had ever heard they had interfered with the course of more or less true love. She explained it by saying that in the days when army posts lay afar from the track of civilization the people were more dependent upon one another, and that then there may have existed Mrs. Hauksbees and Mrs. Knowles, but that to-day the railroads brought in fresh air and ideas from all over the country, and that the officers were constantly being exchanged, and others coming and going on detached service, and that visitors from the bigger outside world were appearing at all times.

The life impresses a stranger as such a peaceful sort of an existence that he thinks that must be its chief and great attraction, and that which makes the army people, as they call themselves, so well content. It sounds rather absurd to speak of an army post of all places in the world as peaceful; but the times are peaceful now, and there is not much work for the officers to do, and they enjoy that blessing which is only to be found in the army and in the Church of Rome—of having one's life laid out for one by others, and in doing what one is told, and in not having to decide things for one's self. You are sure of your home, of your income, and you know exactly what is going to be your work a month or five years later. You are not dependent on the rise of a certain stock, nor the slave of patients or clients, and you have more or less responsibility according to your rank, and responsibility is a thing every man loves. If he has that, and his home and children, a number of congenial people around him, and good hunting and fishing, it would seem easy for him to be content. It is different with his wife. She may unconsciously make life very pleasant for her husband or very uncomfortable, in ways that other women may not. If she leaves him and visits the East to see the new gowns, or the new operas, or her own people, she is criticised as not possessing a truly wifely spirit, and her husband is secretly pitied; and he knows it, and resents it for his wife's sake. While, on the other hand, if she remains always at the post, he is called a selfish fellow, and his wife's people at home in the East think ill of him for keeping her all to himself in *that* wilderness.

The most surprising thing about the frontier army posts, to my mind, was the amount of comfort and the number of pretty trifles one found in the houses, especially when one considered the distance these trifles — such as billiard-tables for the club or canteen, and standing-lamps for the houses on the line — had come. At several dinners, at posts I had only reached after two days' journey by stage, the tables were set exactly as they would have been in New York City with Sherry's men in the kitchen. There were red candle-shades, and salted almonds and ferns in silver centre-pieces, and more forks than one ever knows what to do with, and all the rest of it. I hope the army people will not resent this, and proudly ask, "What did he expect to find?" but I am sure that is not the idea of a frontier post we have received in the East. There was also something delightfully novel in the table-talk, and in hearing

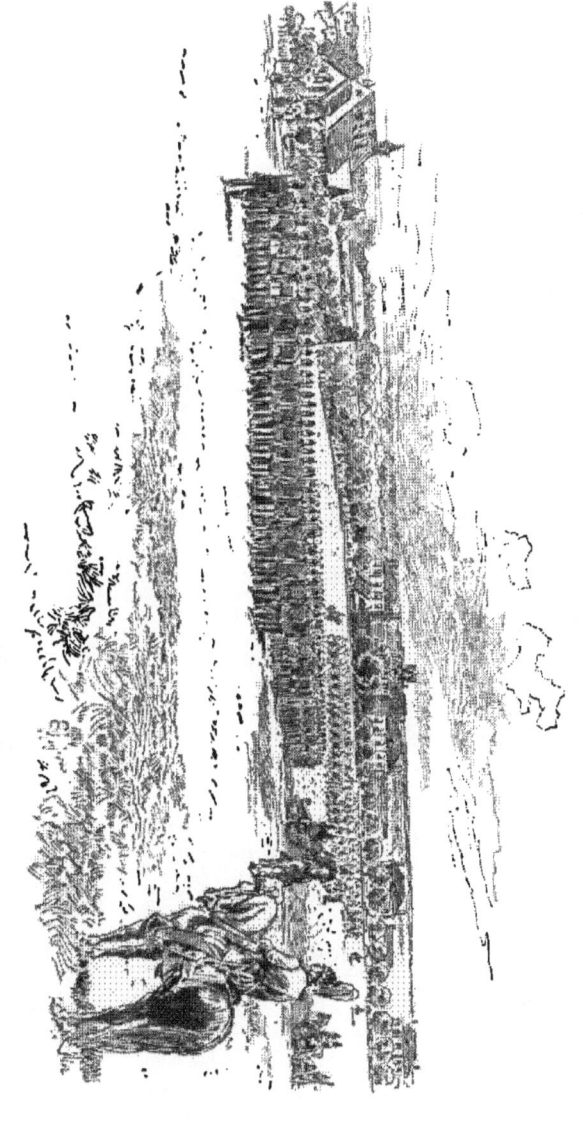
UNITED STATES MILITARY POST—INFANTRY PARADE

one pretty, slight woman, in a smart *décolleté* gown, casually tell how her husband and his men had burned the prairie grass around her children and herself, and turned aside a prairie fire that towered and roared around them, and another of how her first child had been seized with convulsions in a stage-coach when they were snow-bound eighty miles from the post and fifty miles from the nearest city, and how she borrowed a clasp-knife from one of the passengers with which he had been cutting tobacco, and lanced the baby's gums, and so saved his life. There was another hostess who startled us by saying, cheerfully, that the month of June at her last post was the most unpleasant in the year, because it was so warm that it sometimes spoiled the ice for skating, and that the snow in April reached to the sloping eaves of the house; also the daughter of an Indian fighter, while pouring out at a tea one day, told calmly of an Indian who had sprung at her with a knife, and seized her horse's head, and whom she had shaken off by lashing the pony on to his hind legs. She could talk the Sioux language fluently, and had lived for the greater part of her life eight hundred miles from a railroad. Is it any wonder you find all the men in an army post married when there are women who can adapt themselves as gracefully to snow-shoes at Fort Brady as to the serious task of giving dinners at Fort Houston?

Fort Sam Houston at San Antonio is one of the three largest posts in the country, and is in consequence one of the heavens towards which the eyes of the army people turn. It is only twenty minutes from the city, and the weather is mild throughout the year, and in the summer there are palm-trees around the houses; and white uniforms—which are unknown to the posts farther north, and

The West from a Car-Window

which are as pretty as they are hard to keep clean—make the parade-ground look like a cricket-field. They have dances at this post twice a month, the regimental band furnishing the music, and the people from town helping out the sets, and the officers in uniforms with red, white, and yellow stripes. A military ball is always very pretty, and the dancing-hall at Houston is decorated on such occasions with guidons and flags, and palms and broad-leaved plants, which grow luxuriously everywhere, and cost nothing. I went directly from this much-desired post to the little one at Oklahoma City, which is a one-company post, and where there are no semi-monthly dances or serenades by the band; but where, on the other hand, the officers do not stumble over an enlisted man at every step who has to be saluted, and who stands still before them, as though he meant to "hold them up" or ask his way, until he is recognized. The post at Oklahoma City is not so badly off, even though it is built of logs and mud, for the town is near by, and the men get leave to visit it when they wish. But it serves to give one an idea of the many other one-company posts scattered in lonely distances along the borders of the frontier, where there are no towns, and where every man knows what the next man is going to say before he speaks—single companies which the Government has dropped out there, and which it has apparently forgotten, as a man forgets the book he has tucked away in his shelf to read on some rainy day. They will probably find they are remembered when the rainy days come. Fort Sill, in the Oklahoma Territory, is one of the eight-company posts. I visited several of these, and liked them better than those nearer the cities; but then I was not stationed there. The people at these smaller isolated posts seem to live more

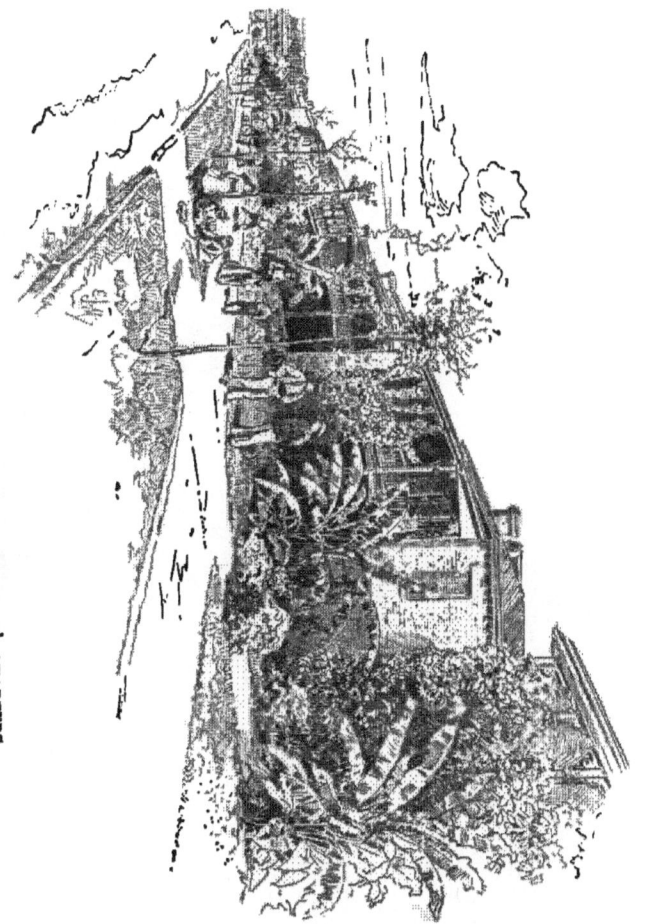

FORT HOUSTON, AT SAN ANTONIO—OFFICERS' QUARTERS

A Civilian at an Army Post

contentedly together. There is not enough of them to separate into cliques or sets, as they did at the larger stations, and they were more dependent one upon another. There was a night when one officer on the line gave a supper, and another (one of his guests) said he wished to contribute the cigars. There had not been an imported cigar in that post for a year at least, and when Captain Ellis brought in a fresh box with *two* paper stamps about it, and the little steamer engraved on the gray band met our eyes, and we knew they had paid the customs duty, there was a most unseemly cheer and undignified haste to have the box opened. And then each man laid his cigar beside his plate, and gazed and sniffed at it, and said "Ah!" and beamed on every one else, and put off lighting it as long as he possibly could. That was a memorable night, and I shall never sufficiently thank Captain Ellis for that cigar, and for showing me how little we of the East appreciate the little things we have always with us, and which become so important when they are taken away.

Fort Sill is really a summer resort; at least, that is what the officers say. I was not there in summer, but it made a most delightful winter resort. There is really no reason at all why people should not go to these interior army posts, as well as to the one at Point Comfort, and spend the summer or winter there, either for their health or for their pleasure. They can reach Fort Sill, for instance, in a three-days' journey from New York, and then there are two days of staging, and you are in a beautiful valley, with rivers running over rocky beds, with the most picturesque Indians all about you, and with red and white flags wigwagging from the parade to the green mountain-tops, and good-

THE BARRACKS, FORT HOUSTON

looking boy-officers to explain the new regulations, and the best of hunting and fishing.

I do not know how the people of Fort Sill will like having their home advertised in this way, but it seems a pity others should not enjoy following Colonel Jones over the prairie after jack-rabbits. We started four of them in one hour, and that is a very good sport when you have a field of twenty men and women and a pack of good hounds. The dogs of Colonel Jones were not as fast as the rabbits, but they were faster than the horses, and so neither dogs nor rabbits were hurt; and that is as it should be, for, as Colonel Jones says, if you caught the rabbits, there would be no more rabbits to catch. Of the serious side of the

A Civilian at an Army Post

life of an army post, of the men and of the families of the men who are away on dangerous field service, I have said nothing, because there was none of it when I was there, nor of the privations of those posts up in the far Northwest, where snow and ice are almost a yearly accompaniment, and where the mail and the papers, which are such a mockery as an exchange for the voices of real people, come only twice a month.

It would be an incomplete story of life at a post which said nothing of the visits of homesickness, which, many strong men in the West have confessed to me, is the worst sickness with which man is cursed. And it is an illness which comes at irregular periods to those of the men who know and who love the East. It is not a homesickness for one home or for one person, but a case of that madness which seized Private Ortheris, only in a less malignant form, and in the officers' quarters. An impotent protest against the immutability of time and of space is one of its symptoms—a sick disgust of the blank prairie, blackened by fire as though it had been drenched with ink, the bare parade-ground, the same faces, the same stories, the same routine and detailed life, which promises no change or end; and with these a longing for streets and rows of houses that seemed commonplace before, of architecture which they had dared to criticise, and which now seems fairer than the lines of the Parthenon, a craving to get back to a place where people, whether one knows them or not, are hurrying home from work under the electric lights, to the rush of the passing hansoms and the cries of the "last editions," and the glare of the shop windows, to the life of a great city that is as careless of the exile's love for it as is the ocean to one who exclaims upon its grandeur from the shore; a soreness of heart which makes men while it lasts put familiar photographs out of sight, which makes the young lieutenants, when the band plays a certain waltz on the parade at sundown, bite their chin-straps, and stare ahead more fixedly than the regulations require. Some officers will confess this to you, and some will not. It is a question which is the happier, he who has no other scenes for which to care, and who is content, or he who eats his heart out for a while, and goes back on leave at last.

VIII

THE HEART OF THE GREAT DIVIDE

VIII

THE HEART OF THE GREAT DIVIDE

THE City of Denver probably does more to keep the Eastern man who is mining or ranching from returning once a year to his own people, and from spending his earnings at home, than any other city in the West. It lays its charm upon him, and stops him half-way, and he decides that the journey home is rather long, and puts it off until the next year, and again until the next, until at last he buys a lot and builds a house, and only returns to the East on his wedding journey. Denver appeals to him more than do any of these other cities, for the reason that the many other Eastern men who have settled there are turning it into a thoroughly Eastern city—a smaller New York in an encircling range of white-capped mountains. If you look up at its towering office buildings, you can easily imagine yourself, were it not for the breadth of the thoroughfare, in down-town New York; and though the glimpse of the mountains at the end of the street in place of the spars and mast-heads of the East and North rivers undeceives you, the mud at your feet serves to help out the delusion. Denver is a really beautiful city, but—and this, I am sure, few people in New York will believe—it has the worst streets in the country. Their mud or their dust, as the season wills it, is the one blot on the city's fair extent; it is as if the City Fathers had served a well-appointed dinner on a soiled table-cloth. But they say they will arrange all that in time.

The two most striking things about the city to me were the public schools and the private houses. Great corporations, insurance companies, and capitalists erect twelve-story buildings everywhere. They do it for an advertisement for themselves or their business, and for the rent of the offices. But these buildings do not in any way represent a city's growth. You will find one or two of such buildings in almost every Western city, but you will find the people who rent the offices in them living in the hotels or in wooden houses on the outskirts. In Denver there are not only the big buildings, but mile after mile of separate houses, and of the prettiest, strictest, and most proper architecture. It is a distinct pleasure to look at these houses, and quite impossible to decide upon the one in which you would rather live. They are not merged together in solid rows, but stand apart, with a little green breathing-space between, each in its turn asserting its own individuality. The greater part of these are built of the peculiarly handsome red stone which is found so plentifully in the Silver State. It is not the red stone which makes them so pleasantly conspicuous, but the taste of the owner or the architect which has turned it to account. As for the public schools, they are more like art museums outside than school-houses; and if as much money and thought in proportion are given to the instruction as have been put upon the buildings, the children of Denver threaten to grow up into a most disagreeably superior class of young persons. Denver possesses those other things which make a city livable, but the public schools and the private houses were to

GATEWAY OF THE GARDEN OF THE GODS, AND PIKE'S PEAK

me the most distinctive features. The Denver Club is quite as handsome and well ordered a club as one would find in New York City, and the University Club, which is for the younger men, brings the wanderers from different colleges very near and pleasantly together. Its members can sing more different college songs in a given space of time than any other body of men I have met. The theatres and the hotels are new and very good, and it is a delight to find servants so sufficiently civilized that the more they are ordered about and the more one gives them to do, the more readily they do it, knowing that this means that they are to be tipped. In the other Western cities, where this pernicious and most valuable institution is apparently unknown, a traveller has to do everything for himself.

You will find that the people of a city always pride themselves on something which the visitor within their gates would fail to notice. They have become familiar with those features which first appeal to him, have outgrown them, and have passed on to admire something else. The citizen of Denver takes a modest pride in the public schools, the private houses, and the great mountains, which seem but an hour's walk distant and are twenty miles away; but he is proudest before all of two things—of his celery and his cable-cars. His celery is certainly the most delicious and succulent that grows, and his cable-cars are very beautiful white and gold affairs, and move with the delightfully terrifying speed of a toboggan. Riding on these cable-cars is one of the institutions of the city, just as in the summer a certain class of young people in New York find their pleasure in driving up and down the Avenue on the top of the omnibuses. But that is a dreary and sentimental journey compared with a ride on the grip-seat of a cable-car, and every one in Denver patronizes this means of locomotion whether on business or on pleasure bent, and whether he has carriages of his own or not. There is not, owing to the altitude, much air to spare in Denver at any time, but when one mounts a cable-car, and is swept with a wild rush around a curve, or dropped down a grade as abruptly as one is dropped down the elevator shaft in the Potter Building, what little air there is disappears, and leaves one gasping. Still, it is a most popular diversion, and even in the winter some of the younger people go cable-riding as we go sleighing, and take lap-robes with them to keep them warm. There is even a "scenic route," which these cars follow, and it is most delightful.

Denver and Colorado Springs pretend to be jealous of one another; why, it is impossible to understand. One is a city, and the other a summer or health resort; and we might as properly compare Boston and Newport, or New York and Tuxedo. In both cities the Eastern man and woman and the English cousin are much more in evidence than the born Western man. These people are very fond of their homes at Denver and at the Springs, but they certainly manage to keep Fifth Avenue and the Sound and the Back Bay prominently in mind. Half of those women whose husbands are wealthy—and every one out here seems to be in that condition—do the greater part of their purchasing along Broadway below Twenty-third Street, their letter-paper is stamped on Union Square, and their husbands are either part or whole owners of a yacht. It sounds very strange to hear them, in a city shut in by ranges of mountain peaks, speak familiarly of Larchmont and Hell Gate and New London and "last year's cruise." Colorado Springs is the great pleasure resort for the whole

The Heart of the Great Divide

State, and the salvation and sometimes the resting-place of a great many invalids from all over the world. It lies at the base of Pike's Peak and Cheyenne Mountain, and is only an hour's drive from the great masses of jagged red rock known as the Garden of the Gods. Pike's Peak, the Garden of the Gods, and the Mount of the Holy Cross are the proudest landmarks in the State. This last mountain was regarded for many years almost as a myth, for while many had seen the formation which gives it its name, no one could place the mountain itself, the semblance of the cross disappearing as one drew near to it. But in 1876 Mr. Hayden, of the Government Survey, and Mr. W. H. Jackson, of Denver, found it, climbed it, and photographed it, and since then artists and others have made it familiar. But it will never become so familiar as to lose aught of its wonderfully impressive grandeur.

There are also near Colorado Springs those mineral waters which give it its name, and of which the people are so proud that they have turned Colorado Springs into a prohibition town, and have made drinking the waters, as it were, compulsory. This is an interesting example of people who support home industries. There is a casino at the Springs, where the Hungarian band plays in summer, a polo field, a manufactured lake for boating, and hundreds of beautiful homes, fashioned after the old English country-house, even to the gate-keeper's lodge and the sun dial on the lawn. And there are cañons that inspire one *not* to attempt to write about them. There are also many English people who have settled there, and who vie with the Eastern visitors in the smartness of their traps and the appearance of their horses. Indeed, both of these cities have so taken on the complexion of the East that one wonders whether it is true that the mining towns of Creede and Leadville lie only twelve hours away, and that one is thousands of miles distant from the City of New York.

It is possible that some one may have followed this series of articles, of which this is the last, from the first, and that he may have decided, on reading them, that the West is filled with those particular people and institutions of which these articles have treated, and that one steps from ranches to army posts, and from Indian reservations to mining camps with easy and uninterrupted interest. This would be, perhaps it is needless to say, an entirely erroneous idea. I only touched on those things which could not be found in the East, and said nothing of the isolation of these particular and characteristic points of interest, of the commonplace and weary distances which lay between them, and of the difficulty of getting from one point to another. For days together, while travelling to reach something of possible interest, I might just as profitably, as far as any material presented itself, have been riding through New Jersey, Pennsylvania, or Ohio. Indians do not necessarily join hands with the cowboys, nor army posts nestle at the feet of mountains filled with silver. The West is picturesque in spots, and, as the dramatic critics say, the interest is not sustained throughout. I confess I had an idea that after I had travelled four days in a straight line due west, every minute of my time would be of value, and that if each man I met was not a character he would tell stories of others who were, and that it would merely be necessary for me to keep my eyes open to have picturesque and dramatic people and scenes pass obligingly before them. I was soon undeceived in this, and learned that in order to reach the West we read about, it would be necessary for

WITHIN THE GATES, GARDEN OF THE GODS

The Heart of the Great Divide

me to leave the railroad, and that I must pay for an hour of interest with days of the most unprofitable travel. Matthew Arnold said, when he returned to England, that he had found this country "uninteresting," and every American was properly indignant; and said he could have forgiven him any adjective but that. If Matthew Arnold travelled from Pittsburg to St. Louis, from St. Louis to Corpus Christi, and from Corpus Christi back through Texas to the Indian Territory, he not only has my sympathy, but I admire him as a descriptive writer. For those who find the level farm lands of Indiana, Illinois, Missouri, Kansas, and the ranches of upper Texas, and the cactus of Southern Texas, and the rolling prairie of the Indian Territory interesting, should travel from Liverpool to London on either line they please to select, and they will understand the Englishman's discontent. Hundreds of miles of level mud and snow followed by a hot and sandy soil and uncultivated farm lands are not as interesting as hedges of hawthorn or glimpses of the Thames or ivy-covered country-houses in parks of oak. The soldiers who guard this land, the Indians who are being crowded out of it, and the cowboys who gallop over it and around their army of cattle, *are* interesting, but they do not stand at the railroad stations to be photographed and to exhibit their peculiar characteristics.

But after one leaves these different States and rides between the mountain ranges of Colorado, he commits a sin if he does not sit day and night by the car window. It is best to say this as it shows the other side of the shield.

You may, while travelling in the West, enjoy the picturesque excitement of being held up by train robbers, but you are in much more constant danger of being held up by commercial travellers and native Western men, who demand that you stand and deliver your name, your past history, your business, and your excuse for being where you are. Neither did I find the West teeming with "characters." I heard of them, and indeed the stories of this or that pioneer or desperado are really the most vivid and most interesting memories I have of the trip. But these men have been crowded out, or have become rich and respectably commonplace, or have been shot, as the case may be. I met the men who had lynched them or who remembered them, but not the men themselves. They no longer over-run the country; they disappeared with the buffalo, and the West is glad of it, but it is disappointing to the visitor. The men I met were men of business, who would rather talk of the new court-house with the lines of the sod still showing around it than of the Indian fights and the killing of the bad men of earlier days when there was no court-house, and when the vigilance committee was a necessary evil. These were "well-posted" and "well-informed" citizens, and if there is one being I dread and fly from, it is a well-posted citizen.

The men who are of interest in the West, and of whom most curious stories might be told, are the Eastern men and the Englishmen who have sought it with capital, or who have been driven there to make their fortunes. Some one once started a somewhat unprofitable inquiry as to what became of all the lost pins. That is not nearly so curious as what becomes of all the living men who drop suddenly out of our acquaintanceship or our lives, and who are not missed, but who are nevertheless lost. I know now what becomes of them; they all go West. I met some men here whom I was sure I had left walking Fifth Avenue, and who told me, on the contrary, that they had been in

POLO ABOVE THE SNOW-LINE AT COLORADO SPRINGS

The Heart of the Great Divide

the West for the last two years. They had once walked Fifth Avenue, but they dropped out of the procession one day, and no one missed them, and they are out here enjoying varying fortunes. The brakesman on a freight and passenger train in Southern Texas was a lower-class man whom I remembered at Lehigh University as an expert fencer; the conductor on the same train was from the same college town; the part owner of a ranch, whom I supposed I had left looking over the papers in the club, told me he had not been in New York for a year, and that his partner was "Jerry" Black, who, as I trust no one has forgotten, was one of Princeton's half-backs, and who I should have said, had any one asked me, was still in Pennsylvania. Another man whom I remembered as a "society" reporter on a New York paper, turned up in a white apron as a waiter at a hotel in ——. I was somewhat embarrassed at first as to whether or not he would wish me to recognize him, but he settled my doubts by winking at me over his heavily-loaded tray, as much as to say it was a very good joke, and that he hoped I was appreciating it to its full value. We met later in the street, and he asked me with the most faithful interest of those whose dances and dinners he had once reported, deprecated a notable scandal among people of the Four Hundred which was filling the papers at that time, and said I could hardly appreciate the pity of such a thing occurring among people of his set. Another man, whom I had known very well in New York, turned up in San Antonio with an entirely new name, wife, and fortune, and verified the tradition which exists there that it is best before one grows to know a man too well, to ask him what was his name *before* he came to Texas. San Antonio seemed particularly rich in histories of those who came there to change their fortunes, and who had changed them most completely. The English gave the most conspicuous examples of these unfortunates—conspicuous in the sense that their position at home had been so good, and their habits of life so widely different.

The proportion of young English gentlemen who are roughing it in the West far exceeds that of the young Americans. This is due to the fact that the former have never been taught a trade or profession, and in consequence, when they have been cheated of the money they brought with them to invest, have nothing but their hands to help them, and so take to driving horses or branding cattle or digging in the streets, as one graduate of Oxford, sooner than write home for money, did in Denver. He is now teaching Greek and Latin in one of our colleges. The manner in which visiting Englishmen are robbed in the West, and the quickness with which some of them take the lesson to heart, and practise it upon the next Englishman who comes out, or upon the prosperous Englishman already there, would furnish material for a book full of pitiful stories. And yet one cannot help smiling at the wickedness of some of these schemes. Three Englishmen, for example, bought, as they supposed, thirty thousand Texas steers; but the Texans who pretended to sell them the cattle drove the same three thousand head ten times around the mountain, as a dozen supers circle around the backdrop of a stage to make an army, and the Englishmen counted and paid for each steer ten times over. There was another Texan who made a great deal of money by advertising to teach young men how to become cowboys, and who charged them ten dollars a month tuition fee, and who set his pupils to work digging holes for fence-posts all over

The Heart of the Great Divide

the ranch, until they grew wise in their generation, and left him for some other ranch, where they were paid thirty dollars per month for doing the same thing. But in many instances it is the tables of San Antonio which take the greater part of the visiting Englishman's money. One gentleman, who for some time represented the Isle of Wight in the Lower House, spent three modest fortunes in the San Antonio gambling-houses, and then married his cook, which proved a most admirable speculation, as she had a frugal mind, and took entire control of his little income. And when the Marquis of Aylesford died in Colorado, the only friend in this country who could be found to take the body back to England was his first-cousin, who at that time was driving a hack around San Antonio. We heard stories of this sort on every side, and we met faro-dealers, cooks, and cowboys who have served through campaigns in India or Egypt, or who hold an Oxford degree. A private in G troop, Third Cavalry, who was my escort on several scouting expeditions in the Garza outfit, was kind enough and quite able to tell me which club in London had the oldest wine-cellar, where one could get the best visiting-cards engraved, and why the Professor of Ancient Languages at Oxford was the superior of the instructor in like studies at Cambridge. He did this quite unaffectedly, and in no way attempted to excuse his present position. Of course, the value of the greater part of these stories depends on the family and personality of the hero, and as I cannot give names, I have to omit the best of them.

There was a little English boy who left San Antonio before I had reached it, but whose name and fame remained behind him. He was eighteen years of age, and just out of Eton, where he had spent all his pocket-money in betting on the races through commissioners. Gambling was his ruling passion at an age when ginger-pop and sweets appealed more strongly to his contemporaries. His people sent him to Texas with four hundred pounds to buy an interest in a ranch, and furnished him with a complete outfit of London-made clothing. An Englishman who saw the boy's box told me he had noted the different garments packed carefully away, just as his mother had placed them, and each marked with his name. The Eton boy lost the four hundred pounds at roulette in the first week after his arrival in San Antonio, and pawned his fine clothes in the next to "get back." He lost all he ventured. At the end of ten days he was peddling fruit around the streets in his bare feet. He made twenty-five cents the first day, and carried it to the gambling-house where he had already lost his larger fortune, and told one of the dealers he would cut the cards with him for the money. The boy cut first, and the dealer won; but the other was enough of a gambler to see that the dealer had stooped to win his last few pennies unfairly. The boy's eyes filled up with tears of indignation.

"You thief!" he cried, "you cheated me!"

The dealer took his revolver from the drawer of the table, and, pointing it at his head, said: "Do you know what we do to people who use that word in Texas? We kill them!"

The boy clutched the table with both hands and flung himself across it so that his forehead touched the barrel of the revolver. "You thief!" he repeated, and so shrilly that every one in the room heard him. "I say you cheated me!"

The gambler lowered the trigger slowly and tossed the pistol back in the drawer. Then he picked up a ten-dollar gold piece and shoved it towards him.

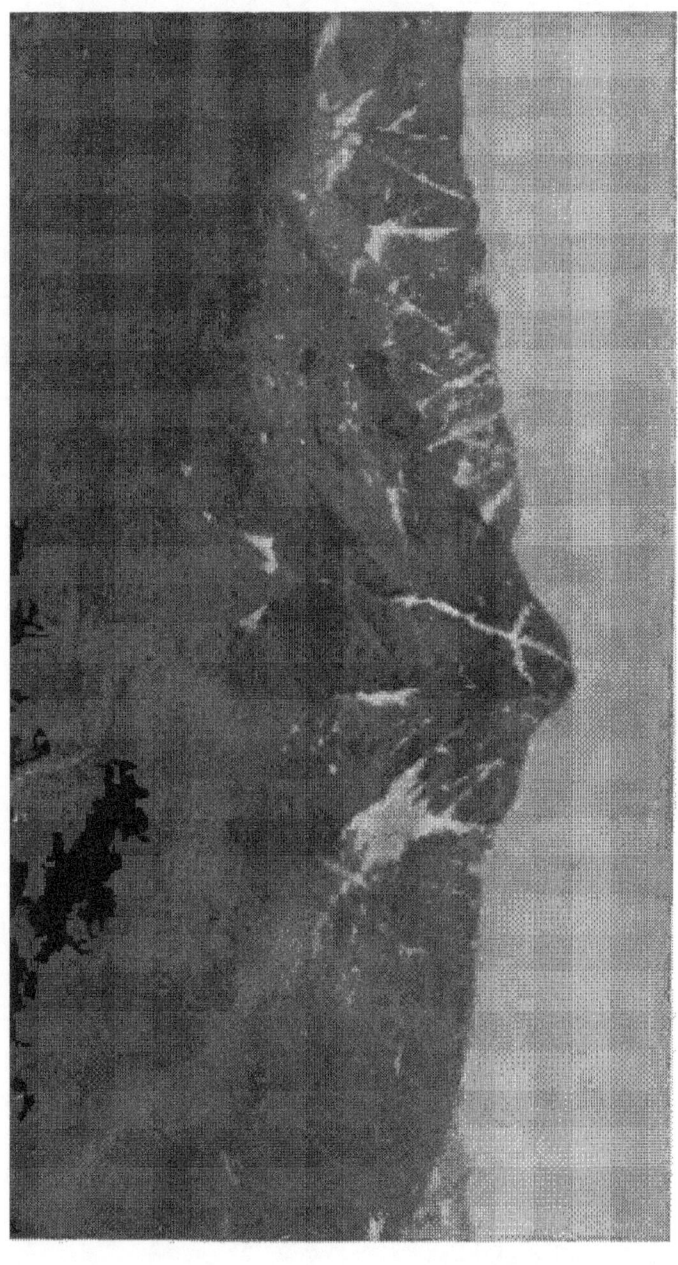

The Heart of the Great Divide

"Here," he said, "that 'll help take you home. You're too damned tough for Texas!"

The other Englishmen in San Antonio filled out the sum and sent him back to England. His people are well known in London; his father is a colonel in the Guards.

The most notable Englishman who ever came to Texas was Ben Thompson; but he arrived there at so early an age, and became so thoroughly Western in his mode of life, that Texans claim him as their own. I imagine, however, he always retained some of the traditions of his birthplace, as there is a story of his standing with his hat off to talk to an English nobleman, when Thompson at the time was the most feared and best known man in all Texas. The stories of his recklessness and ignorance of fear, and utter disregard of the value of others' lives as well as his own, are innumerable. A few of them are interesting and worth keeping, as they show the typical bad man of the highest degree in his different humors, and also as I have not dared to say half as much about bad men as I should have liked to do. Thompson killed eighteen men in different parts of Texas, and was for this made marshal of Austin, on the principle that if he must kill somebody, it was better to give him authority to kill other desperadoes than reputable citizens. As marshal it was his pleasure to pull up his buggy across the railroad track just as the daily express train was about to start, and covering the engineer with his revolver, bid him hold the train until he was ready to move on. He would then call some trembling acquaintance from the crowd on the platform and talk with him leisurely, until he thought he had successfully awed the engineer and established his authority. Then he would pick up his reins and drive on, saying to the engineer, "You needn't think, sir, any corporation can hurry me." The position of the unfortunate man to whom he talked must have been most trying, with a locomotive on one side and a revolver on the other.

One day a cowboy, who was a well-known bully and a would-be desperado, shot several bullet-holes through the high hat of an Eastern traveller who was standing at the bar of an Austin hotel. Thompson heard of this, and, purchasing a high hat, entered the bar-room.

"I hear," he said, facing the cowboy, "that you are shooting plug-hats here to-day; perhaps you would like to take a shot at mine." He then raised his revolver and shot away the cowboy's ear. "I meant," he said, "to hit your ear; did I do it?" The bully showed proof that he had. "Well, then," said the marshal, "get out of here;" and catching the man by his cartridge-belt, he threw him out into the street, and so put an end to his reputation as a desperate character forever.

Thompson was naturally unpopular with a certain class in the community. Two barkeepers who had a personal grudge against him, with no doubt excellent reason, lay in ambush for him behind the two bars of the saloon, which stretched along either wall. Thompson entered the room from the street in ignorance of any plot against him until the two men halted him with shot-guns. They had him so surely at their pleasure that he made no effort to reach his revolver, but stood looking from one to the other, and smiling grimly. But his reputation was so great, and their fear of him so actual, that both men missed him, although not twenty feet away, and with shot-guns in their hands. Then Thompson took out his pistol deliberately and killed them.

A few years ago he became involved in San Antonio with

"Jack" Harris, the keeper of a gambling-house and variety theatre. Harris lay in wait for Thompson behind the swinging doors of his saloon, but Thompson, as he crossed the Military Plaza, was warned of Harris's hiding-place, and shot him through the door. He was tried for the murder, and acquitted on the ground of self-defence; and on his return to Austin was met at the station by a brass band and all the fire companies. Perhaps inspired by this, he returned to San Antonio, and going to Harris's theatre, then in the hands of his partner, Joe Foster, called from the gallery for Foster to come up and speak to him. Thompson had with him a desperado named King Fisher, and against him every man of his class in San Antonio, for Harris had been very popular. Foster sent his assistant, a very young man named Bill Sims, to ask Thompson to leave the place, as he did not want trouble.

"I have come to have a reconciliation," said Thompson. "I want to shake hands with my old friend, Joe Foster. Tell him I won't leave till I see him, and I won't make a row."

Sims returned with Foster, and Thompson held out his hand.

"Joe," he said, "I have come all the way from Austin to shake hands with you. Let's make up, and call it off."

"I can't shake hands with you, Ben," Foster said. "You killed my partner, and you know well enough I am not the sort to forget it. Now go, won't you, and don't make trouble."

Thompson said he would leave in a minute, but they must drink together first. There was a bar in the gallery, which was by this time packed with men who had learned of Thompson's presence in the theatre, but Fisher and

Thompson stood quite alone beside the bar. The marshal of Austin looked up and saw Foster's glass untouched before him, and said,

"Aren't you drinking with me, Joe?"

Foster shook his head.

"Well, then," cried Thompson, "the man who won't drink with me, nor shake hands with me, fights me."

He reached back for his pistol, and some one—a jury of twelve intelligent citizens decided it was not young Bill Sims—shot him three times in the forehead. They say you could have covered the three bullet-holes with a half-dollar. But so great was the desperate courage of this ruffian that even as he fell he fired, holding his revolver at his hip, and killing Foster, and then, as he lay on his back, with every nerve jerking in agony, he emptied his revolver into the floor, ripping great gashes in the boards about him. And so he died, as he would have elected to die, with his boots on, and with the report of his pistol the last sound to ring in his ears. King Fisher was killed at the same moment; and the *Express* spoke of it the next morning as "A Good Night's Work."

I had the pleasure of meeting Mr. Sims at the gambling palace, which was once Harris's, then Foster's, and which is now his, and found him a jolly, bright-eyed young man of about thirty, with very fine teeth, and a most contagious laugh. He was just back from Dwight, and told us of a man who had been cured there, and who had gone away with his mother leaning on his arm, and what this man had said to them of his hopes for the future when he left; and as he told it the tears came to his eyes, and he coughed, and began to laugh over a less serious story. I tried all the time to imagine him, somewhat profanely, I am afraid, as a

PIKE'S PEAK FROM COLORADO SPRINGS

The Heart of the Great Divide

young David standing up before this English giant, who had sent twoscore of other men out of the world, and to picture the glaring, crowded gallery, with the hot air and smoke, and the voice of the comic singer rising from the stage below, and this boy and the marshal of Austin facing one another with drawn revolvers; but it was quite impossible.

There are a great many things one only remembers to say as the train is drawing out of the station, and which have to be spoken from the car window. And now that my train is so soon to start towards the East, I find there are many things which it seems most ungracious to leave unsaid. I should like to say much of the hospitality of the West. We do not know such hospitality in the East. A man brings us a letter of introduction there, and we put him up at the club we least frequently visit, and regret that he should have come at a time when ours is so particularly crowded with unbreakable engagements. It is not so here. One might imagine the Western man never worked at all, so entirely is his time yours, if you only please to claim it. And from the first few days of my trip to the last, this self-effacement of my hosts and eagerness to please accompanied me wherever I went. It was the same in every place, whether in army posts or ranches, or among that most delightful coterie of the Denver Club "who never sleep," or on the border of Mexico, where "Bob" Haines, the sheriff of Zepata County, Texas, before he knew who I or my soldier escort might be, and while we were still but dust-covered figures in the night, rushed into the house and ordered a dinner and beds for us, and brought out his last two bottles of beer. The sheriff of Zepata County, "who can shoot with both hands," need bring no letter of introduction with him if he will deign to visit me when he comes to New York. And as for that Denver Club coterie, they already know that the New York clubs are also supplied with electric buttons.

And now that it is at an end, I find it hard to believe that I am not to hear again the Indian girls laughing over their polo on the prairie, or the regimental band playing the men on to the parade, and that I am not to see the officers' wives watching them from the line at sunset, as the cannon sounds its salute and the flag comes fluttering down.

And yet New York is not without its good points.

If any one doubts this, let him leave it for three months, and do one-night stands at fourth-rate hotels, or live on alkali water and bacon, and let him travel seven thousand miles over a country where a real-estate office, a Citizen's Bank, and Quick Order Restaurant, with a few surrounding houses, make, as seen from the car window, a booming city, where beautiful scenery and grand mountains are separated by miles of prairie and chaparral, and where there is no Diana of the Tower nor bronze Farragut to greet him daily as he comes back from work through Madison Square. He will then feel a love for New York equal to the Chicagoan's love for *his* city, and when he sees across the New Jersey flats the smoke and the tall buildings and the twin spires of the cathedral, he will wish to shout, as the cowboys do when they "come into town," at being back again in the only place where one can both hear the Tough Girl of the East Side ask for her shoes, and the horn of the Country Club's coach tooting above the roar of the Avenue.

The West is a very wonderful, large, unfinished, and out-of-doors portion of our country, and a most delightful place to *visit*. I would advise every one in the East to visit it, and I hope to revisit it myself. Some of those who go will not only visit it, but will make their homes there, and the course of empire will eventually Westward take its way. But when it does, it will leave one individual behind it clinging closely to the Atlantic seaboard.

Little old New York is good enough for him.

THE END

www.ingramcontent.com/pod-product-compliance
Lightning Source LLC
Chambersburg PA
CBHW020406230426
43664CB00009B/1202